CUT AND CREATE!

ON THE FARM

EASY STEP-BY-STEP PROJECTS THAT TEACH SCISSOR SKILLS

Teaching & Learning Company

1204 Buchanan St., P.O. Box 10

Carthage, IL 62321

This book belongs to

_____

This book was developed for the Teaching & Learning Company
by The Good Neighbor Press, Inc., Grand Junction, CO.

ISBN No. 1-57310-019-6

Printing No. 987654321

Teaching & Learning Company
1204 Buchanan St., P.O. Box 10
Carthage, IL 62321

TABLE OF CONTENTS

Dear Teacher or Parent,

Cut and Create! On the Farm was developed to provide you, the parent or classroom teacher, with activities that will serve your young children in two ways:

1) provide easy step-by-step projects that develop scissor skills and reinforce visual-motor coordination, and

2) supplement your art program with activities that are fun and colorful, have great display possibilities and use materials that are readily available.

Amazingly simple, fun activities like the ones included in this book will help your early childhood students build a solid foundation for well-developed information processing skills. The process of completing a *Cut and Create* activity will require your students to observe and discriminate the separate parts of the figure they're creating and their relationship to one another. Each activity becomes an enjoyable challenge to generate cognitive knowledge!

Structured, sequential activities are *not* intended to take the place of a developmentally appropriate process-oriented art program. However, these scissor skill activities are very useful in achieving the following:

• Developing manual dexterity and patterns of movement

• Encouraging social communicability

• Helping the child to master his environment by controlling tools and materials

• Encouraging observation

• Developing discrimination of color, shape and texture

• Stimulating students' imaginations

• Developing skills necessary for mathematical thinking such as grouping, ordering and spatial orientation

We hope you and your students enjoy the scissor skill activities in *Cut and Create!* They're simple, easy to implement and fun to create!

Materials: *yellow, red, blue, pink, white and black paper; scissors; glue; broom straw*
Optional Materials: *wallpaper sample books and yarn*

SCARECROW

1 Cut one #1 head from yellow paper. Cut one #2 collar from red paper. Glue the head to the collar as shown.

2 Cut one #3 mouth from black paper. Cut two #4 eyes from white paper. Glue them to the head as shown.

3 Cut two #5 eyes from black paper. Cut one #6 nose from red paper. Glue as shown.

4 Cut one #7 hat from blue paper and glue to the top of the head, above the eyes.

5 Cut two #8 cheeks from pink or orange paper. Cut two #9 teeth from white paper. Glue them as shown.

6 **Optional:** Add patterned patches cut from wallpaper book. Add a bow tied from yarn. Use a drop of glue to attach it to the chin. Glue three or four pieces of broom straw to the underside of the hat.

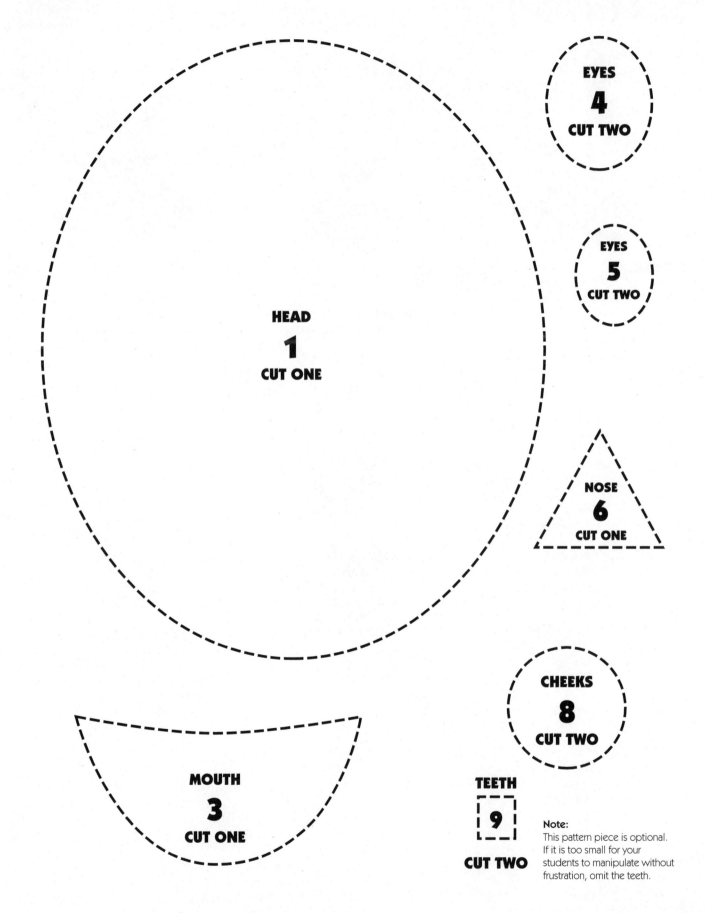

EYES
4
CUT TWO

EYES
5
CUT TWO

HEAD
1
CUT ONE

NOSE
6
CUT ONE

CHEEKS
8
CUT TWO

MOUTH
3
CUT ONE

TEETH
9
CUT TWO

Note:
This pattern piece is optional. If it is too small for your students to manipulate without frustration, omit the teeth.

SCARECROW PATTERNS

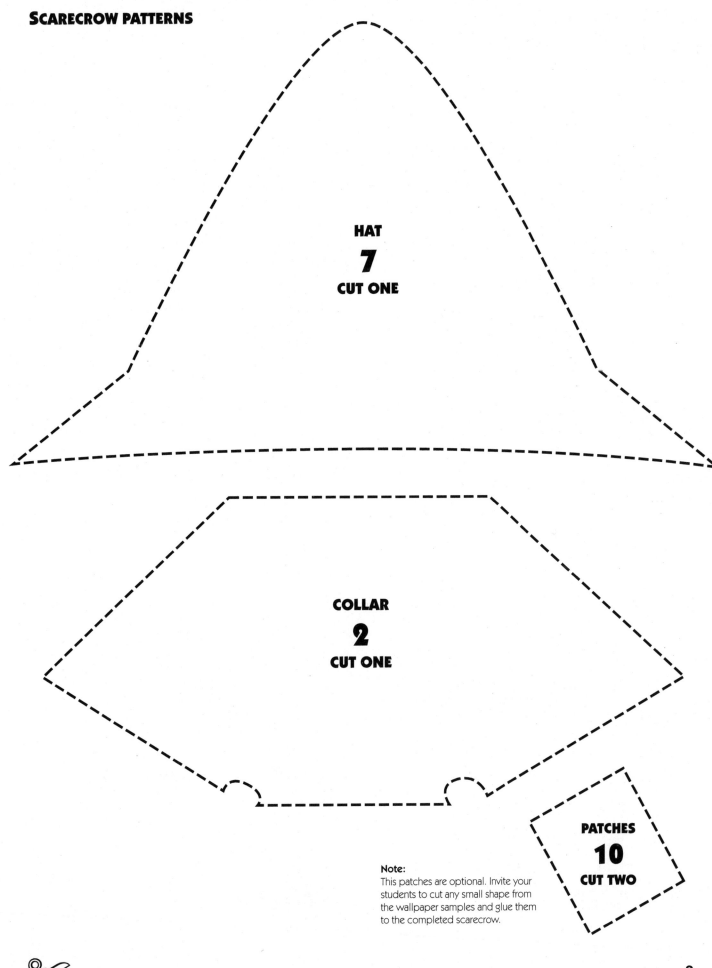

HAT
7
CUT ONE

COLLAR
2
CUT ONE

PATCHES
10
CUT TWO

Note:
This patches are optional. Invite your students to cut any small shape from the wallpaper samples and glue them to the completed scarecrow.

Materials: *multicultural-colored paper; blue, white, yellow and black paper; scissors; glue; black marker or crayon; yarn*

FARM CHILD

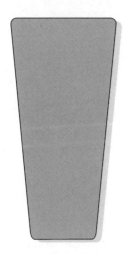

1 Cut one #1 body from blue paper. Cut one #2 head from multicultural-colored paper. Cut one #3 smile from black paper. Glue the smile to the face as shown.

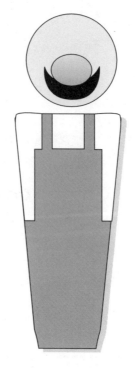

2 Cut one #4 nose from colored paper. Glue it to the head as shown. Cut two #5 arms from white paper. Cut one #6 shirt from white paper. Glue these pieces to the body as shown.

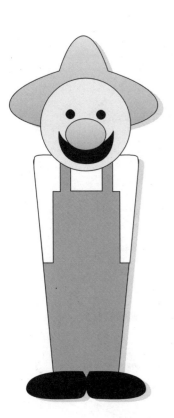

3 Cut one #7 hat from yellow paper. Glue this piece to the underside of the head as shown. Cut two #8 shoes from black paper. Glue them to the body as shown. Using a black marker or crayon, color eyes as shown.

4 Cut two #9 hands from colored paper to match the face. Glue them to the body as shown. Cut pieces of yarn. Glue the pieces onto the head to create hair.

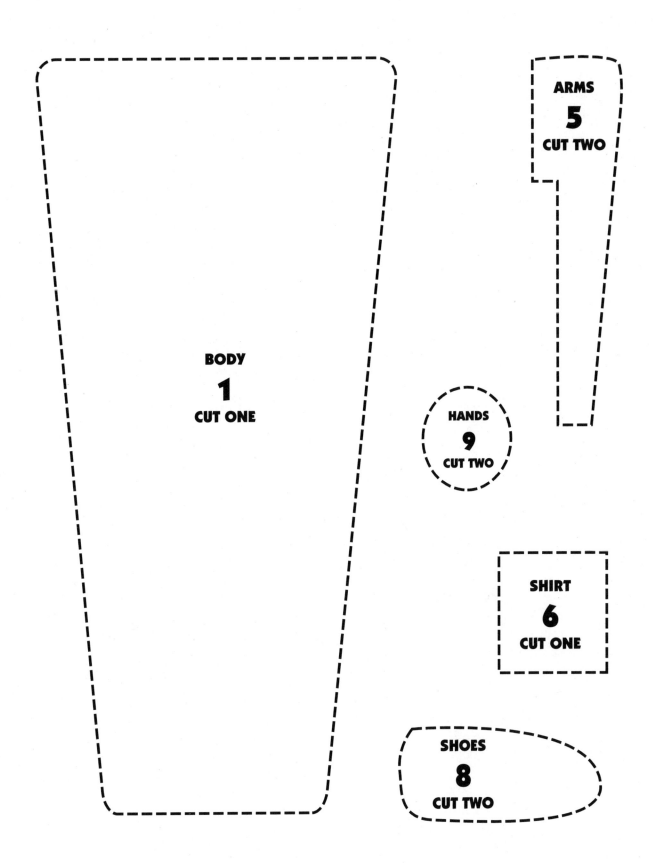

ARMS
5
CUT TWO

BODY
1
CUT ONE

HANDS
9
CUT TWO

SHIRT
6
CUT ONE

SHOES
8
CUT TWO

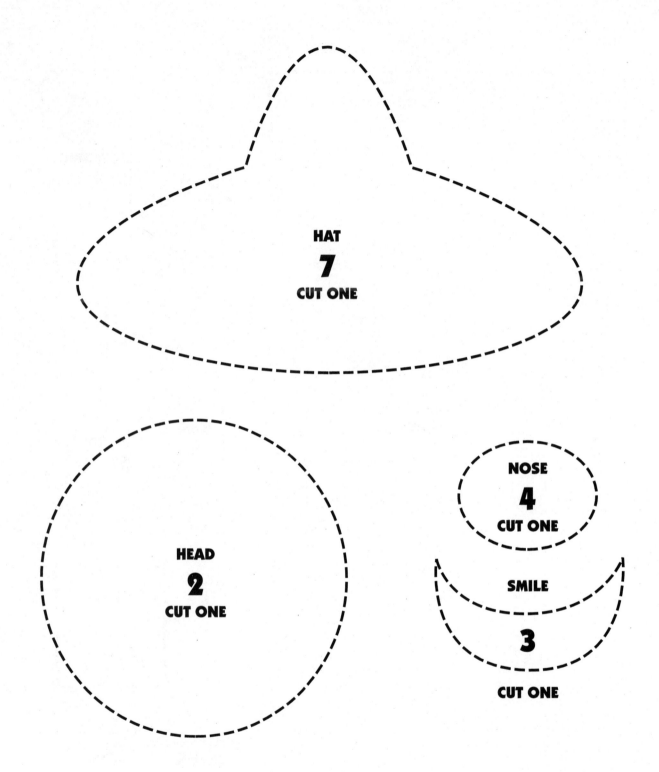

HAT
7
CUT ONE

HEAD
2
CUT ONE

NOSE
4
CUT ONE

SMILE
3
CUT ONE

Materials: *pink, red and black paper; scissors; glue; black crayon or marker*

PIG

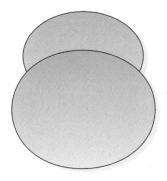

1 Cut one #1 head from pink paper. Cut one #9 face from pink paper. Glue it to the #1 head as shown.

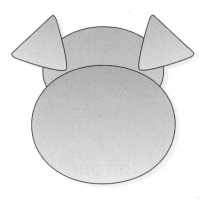

2 Cut two #3 ears from pink paper. Glue them to the head as shown.

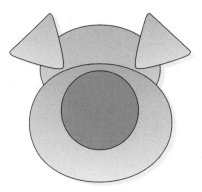

3 Cut one #4 nose from red paper. Glue it to the face as shown.

4 Cut one #5 nose from pink paper. Glue it, centered, to the #4 nose. Cut one #6 mouth from black paper. Glue it to the pig's face as shown.

5 Cut four #7 circles from black paper. Glue two of the circles to the nose as shown and two of the circles to the head as shown.

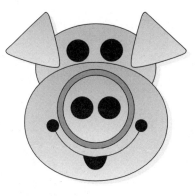

6 With black crayon or marker, add a wide smile to your new farm friend!

Pig Patterns

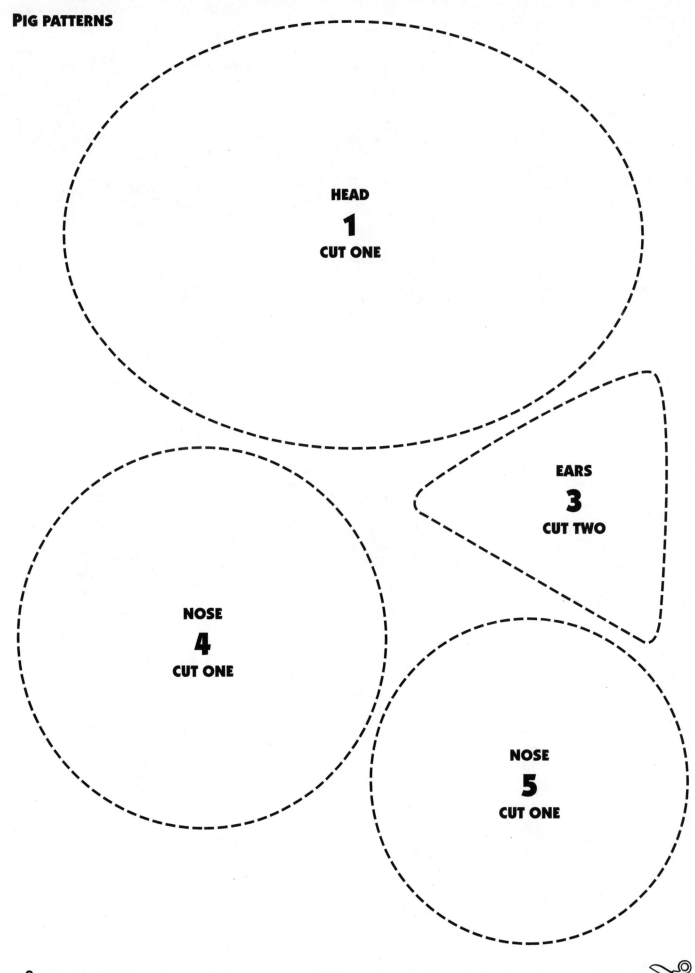

HEAD
1
CUT ONE

EARS
3
CUT TWO

NOSE
4
CUT ONE

NOSE
5
CUT ONE

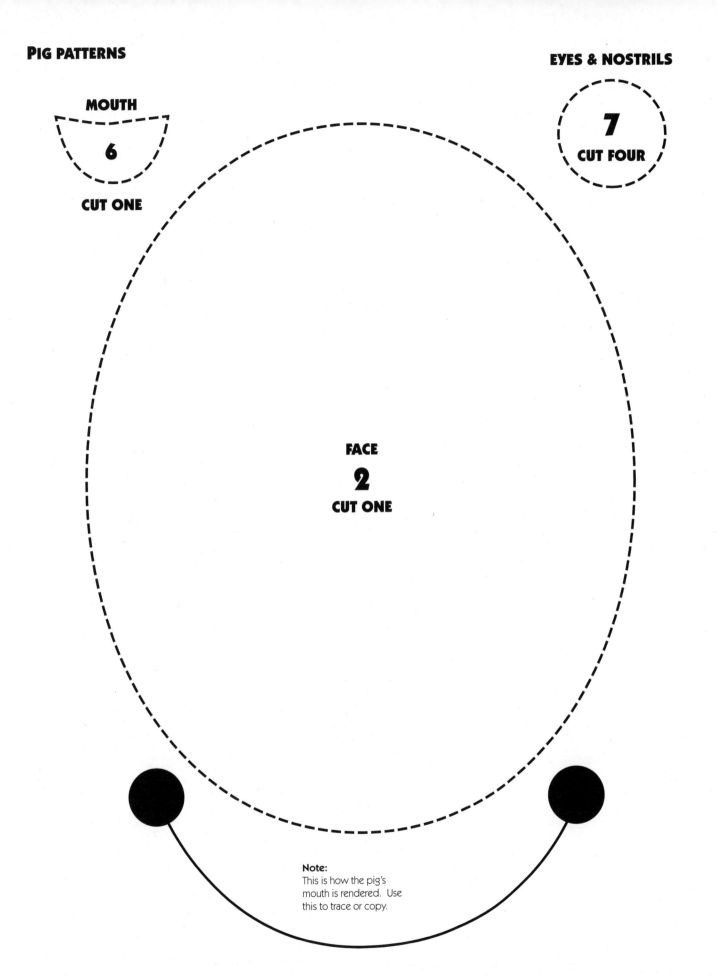

PIG PATTERNS

EYES & NOSTRILS

MOUTH

6

CUT ONE

7

CUT FOUR

FACE

2

CUT ONE

Note:
This is how the pig's
mouth is rendered. Use
this to trace or copy.

PIG PATTERNS

COW

Materials: beige, brown, black and white paper; scissors; glue

▼ **1** Cut one #1 head from beige paper. Cut one #2 muzzle from beige paper. Glue the muzzle to the head as shown.

▼ **2** Cut one #3 mouth from brown paper. Glue it to the underside of the muzzle as shown. Cut one #4 hair pattern from brown paper. Glue it to the head as shown.

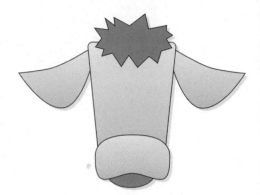

▼ **3** Cut two #5 ears from beige paper. Glue them to the underside of the head as shown.

▼ **4** Cut two #6 nostrils from beige paper. Glue them to the top of the muzzle as shown. Cut two #7 horns from white paper. Glue them to the underside of the head as shown.

▼ **5** Cut two #8 nostrils from black paper. Glue them to the #6 nostrils as shown.

▼ **6** Cut two #9 eyes from black paper. Glue them to the head as shown. "Moo!"

COW PATTERNS

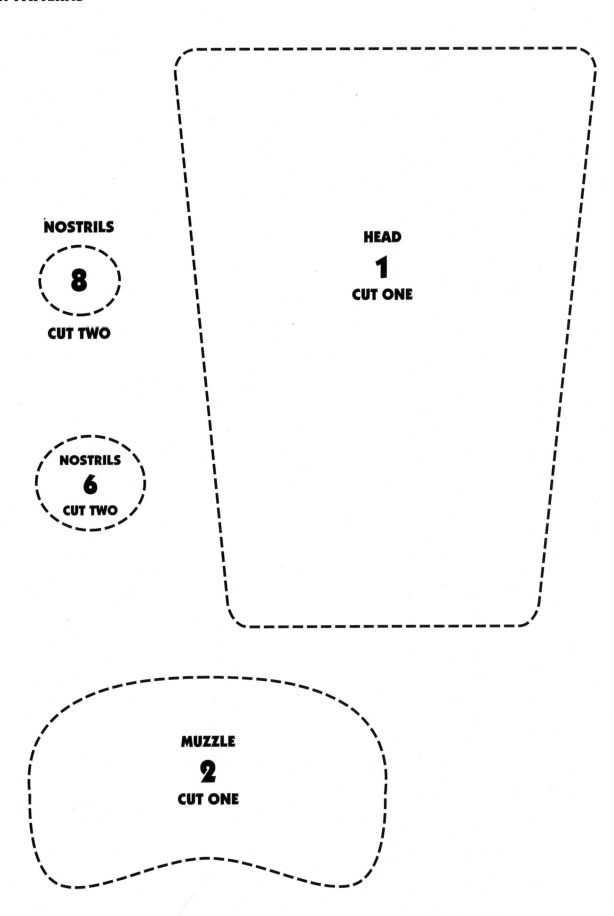

NOSTRILS

8

CUT TWO

HEAD

1

CUT ONE

NOSTRILS

6

CUT TWO

MUZZLE

2

CUT ONE

COW PATTERNS

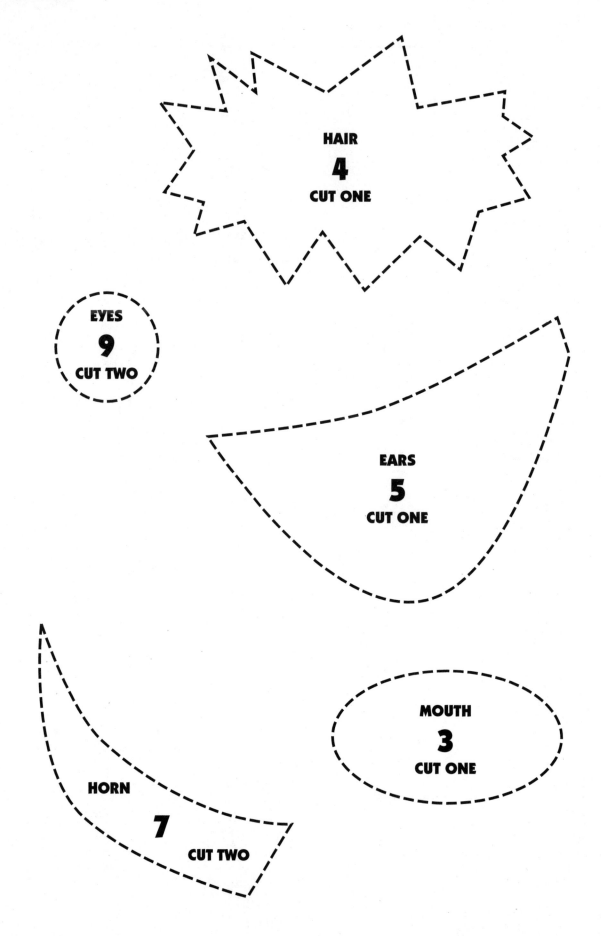

HAIR
4
CUT ONE

EYES
9
CUT TWO

EARS
5
CUT ONE

MOUTH
3
CUT ONE

HORN
7
CUT TWO

CALF

Materials: *light brown or beige paper, black paper, scissors, glue, black crayon or marker*

1 Cut one #1 head from beige paper.

2 Cut one #2 forehead from beige paper. Glue it on top of the #1 head as shown.

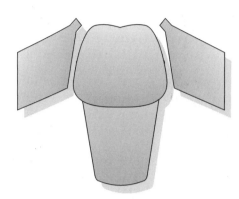

3 Cut two #3 ears from beige paper.

4 Cut two #4 ears from black paper. Glue them, centered, to the beige ears. Cut one #5 nose from black paper. Glue it to the head as shown.

5 Glue the ears to the head as shown. Cut two #6 eyes from black paper. Glue them to the forehead as shown.

6 With a black crayon or marker, add a smile on either side of the nose as shown.

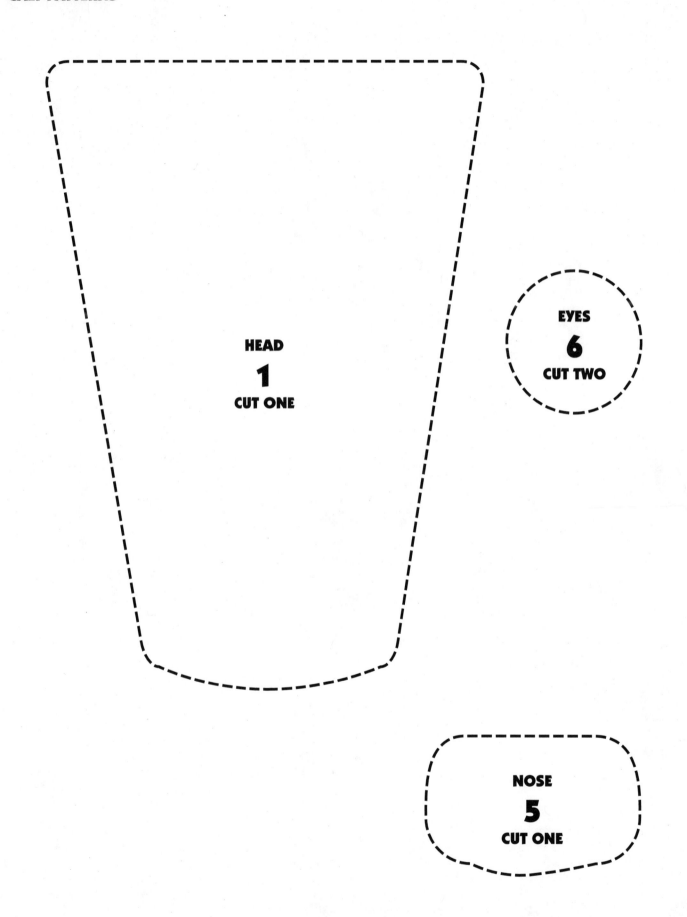

HEAD

1

CUT ONE

EYES

6

CUT TWO

NOSE

5

CUT ONE

CALF PATTERNS

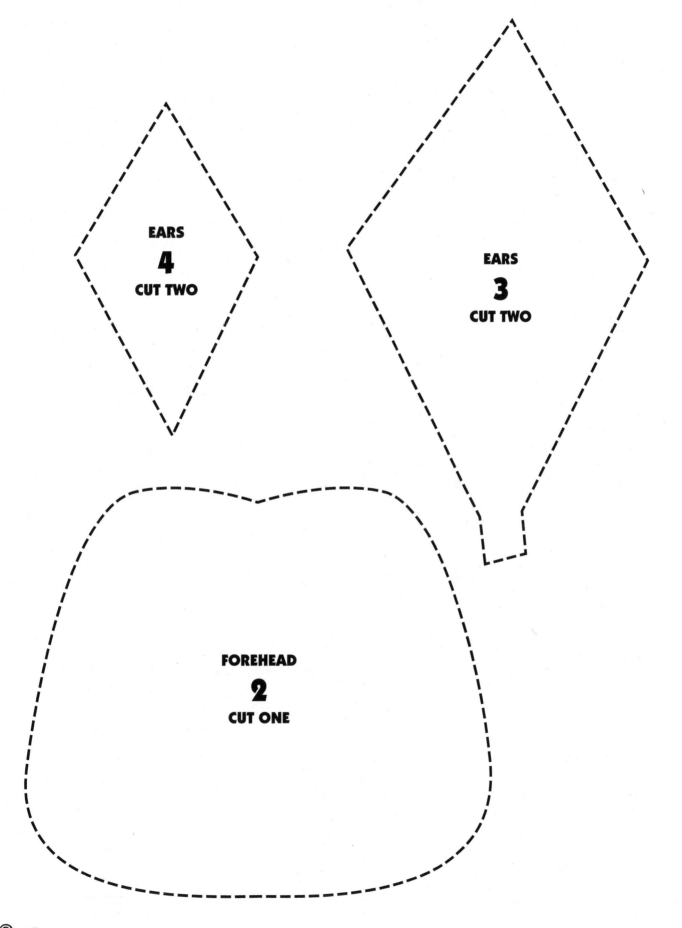

EARS
4
CUT TWO

EARS
3
CUT TWO

FOREHEAD
2
CUT ONE

Materials: *beige, brown, black and white paper; scissors; glue; yarn; black crayon or marker*

BISON

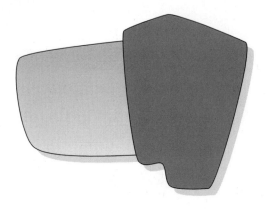

▼**1** Cut one #1 body from beige paper. Cut one #2 body from brown paper. Glue it to the #1 body as shown.

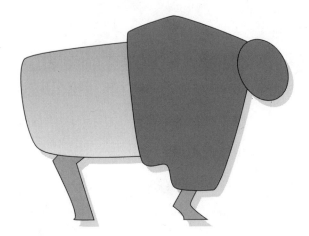

▼**2** Cut one #3 back leg and one #4 front leg from brown paper. Glue them to the underside of the body as shown. Cut one #5 head from brown paper and glue it to the front of the body as shown.

▼**3** Cut one #6 head from beige paper. Cut one #7 nose from black paper. Glue the nose to the head as shown. Cut one #8 horn from white paper. Glue the horn to the top of the head as shown.

▼**4** Cut a piece of yarn 4" to 5" (10.16 to 12.7 cm) long. Glue it to the bison with a drop of glue. Add an eye and a smile with black crayon or marker. Glue a 3" to 4" (7.62 to 10.16 cm) piece of yarn to create a tail for your bison.

BISON PATTERNS

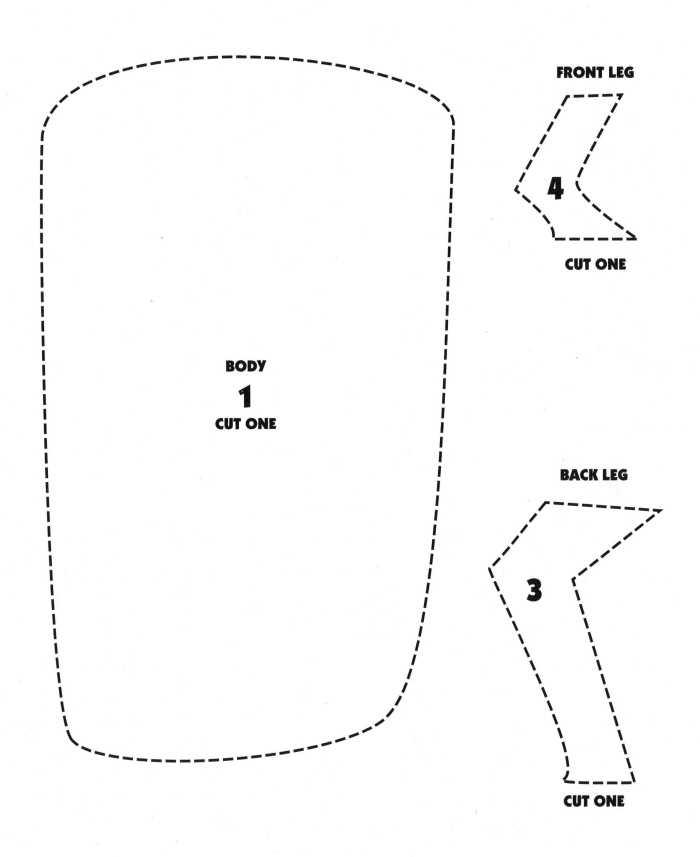

FRONT LEG

4

CUT ONE

BODY

1

CUT ONE

BACK LEG

3

CUT ONE

BISON PATTERNS

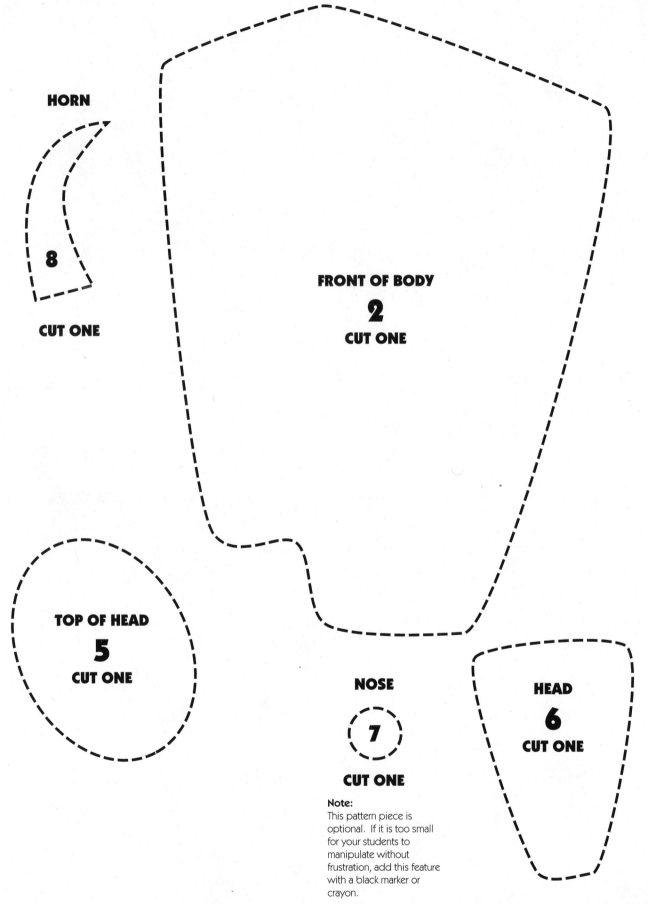

HORN

8

CUT ONE

FRONT OF BODY
2
CUT ONE

TOP OF HEAD
5
CUT ONE

NOSE
7
CUT ONE

HEAD
6
CUT ONE

Note:
This pattern piece is
optional. If it is too small
for your students to
manipulate without
frustration, add this feature
with a black marker or
crayon.

Materials: *brown, white and black paper; scissors; glue; black crayon or marker*

KID

 Cut one #1 head from brown paper.

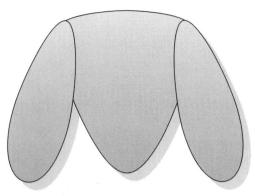

2 Cut two #2 ears from brown paper. Glue them to the sides of the head as shown.

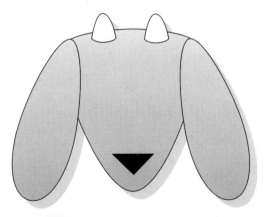

3 Cut one #3 nose from black paper. Glue it to the head. Cut two #4 horns from white paper. Glue them to the top of the head as shown.

4 Cut two #5 eyes from black paper. Glue them to the head as shown. With a black crayon or marker, add the mouth to the kid.

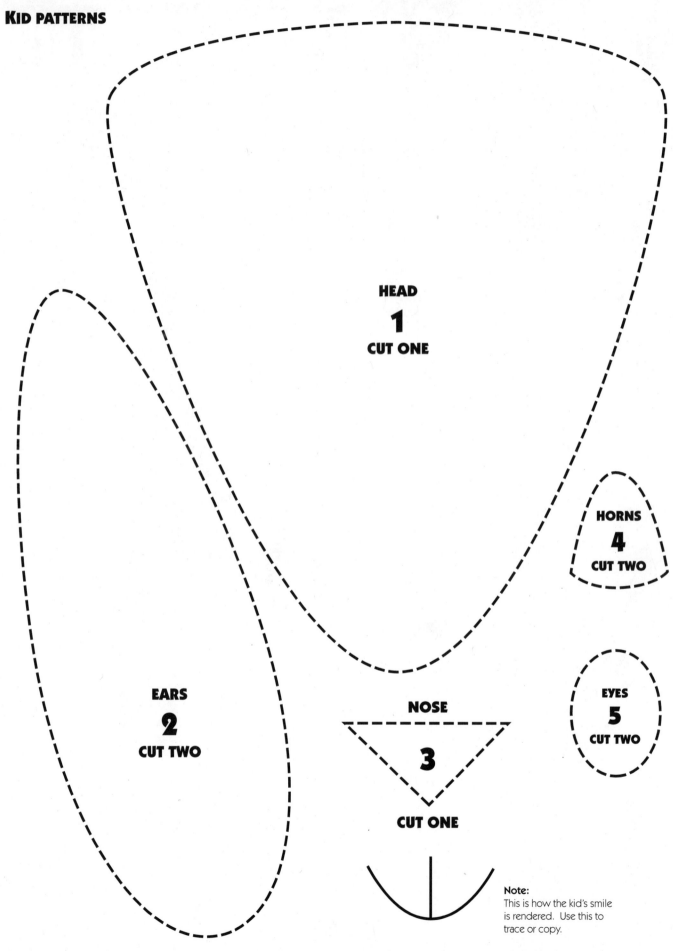

HEAD

1

CUT ONE

HORNS

4

CUT TWO

EARS

2

CUT TWO

NOSE

3

CUT ONE

EYES

5

CUT TWO

Note:
This is how the kid's smile is rendered. Use this to trace or copy.

Materials: *black and gray paper, scissors, glue, black crayon or marker*

DONKEY

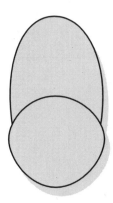

1 Cut one #1 head from gray paper. Cut one #2 muzzle from gray paper. Glue the muzzle to the head as shown.

2 Cut one #3 mane from black paper. Glue it to the top of the donkey's head.

3 Cut two #4 eyes from black paper. Glue the eyes to the head as shown.

4 Cut two #5 ears from gray paper. Cut two #6 ears from black paper. Glue the #6 ears, centered, to the #5 ears.

5 Glue the ears to the underside of the donkey's head.

6 Cut two #7 nostrils from black paper. Glue them to the muzzle as shown. Add a smile using black crayon or marker.

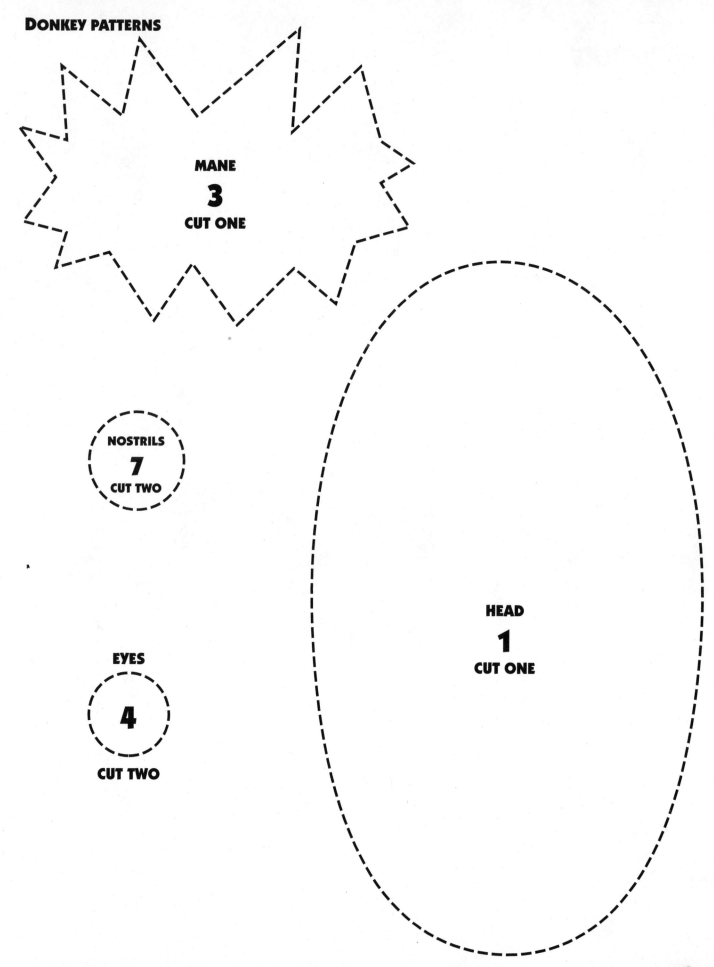

DONKEY PATTERNS

MANE
3
CUT ONE

NOSTRILS
7
CUT TWO

EYES
4
CUT TWO

HEAD
1
CUT ONE

DONKEY PATTERNS

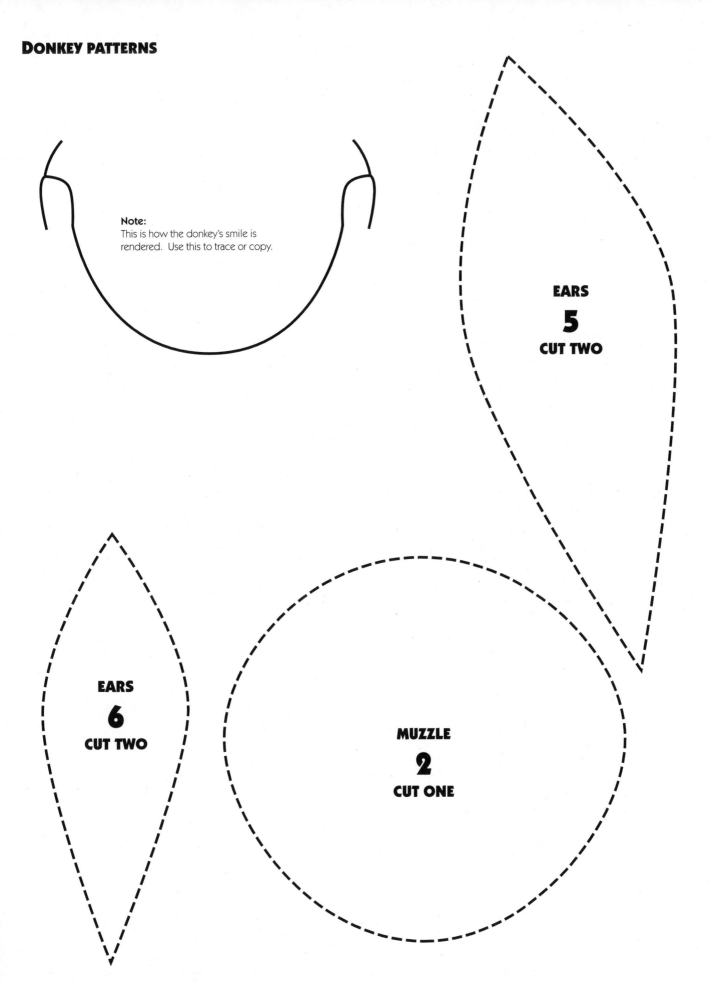

Note:
This is how the donkey's smile is rendered. Use this to trace or copy.

EARS
5
CUT TWO

EARS
6
CUT TWO

MUZZLE
2
CUT ONE

LAMB

Materials: *white, gray and black paper; scissors; glue; black crayon or marker (If you would like a more fanciful version, use light blue paper instead of gray paper.)*

 Cut one #1 head from white paper.

2 Cut one #2 face from gray paper. Glue it to the #1 head as shown.

3 Cut two #3 ears from white paper. Glue them to the head as shown.

4 Cut two #4 ears from black paper. Glue them, centered, to the #3 ears.

5 Cut two #5 eyes from black paper. Glue them to the face and head as shown.

6 Cut one #6 nose from black paper. Glue it to the face as shown. With a black crayon or marker, add a smile to the face as shown.

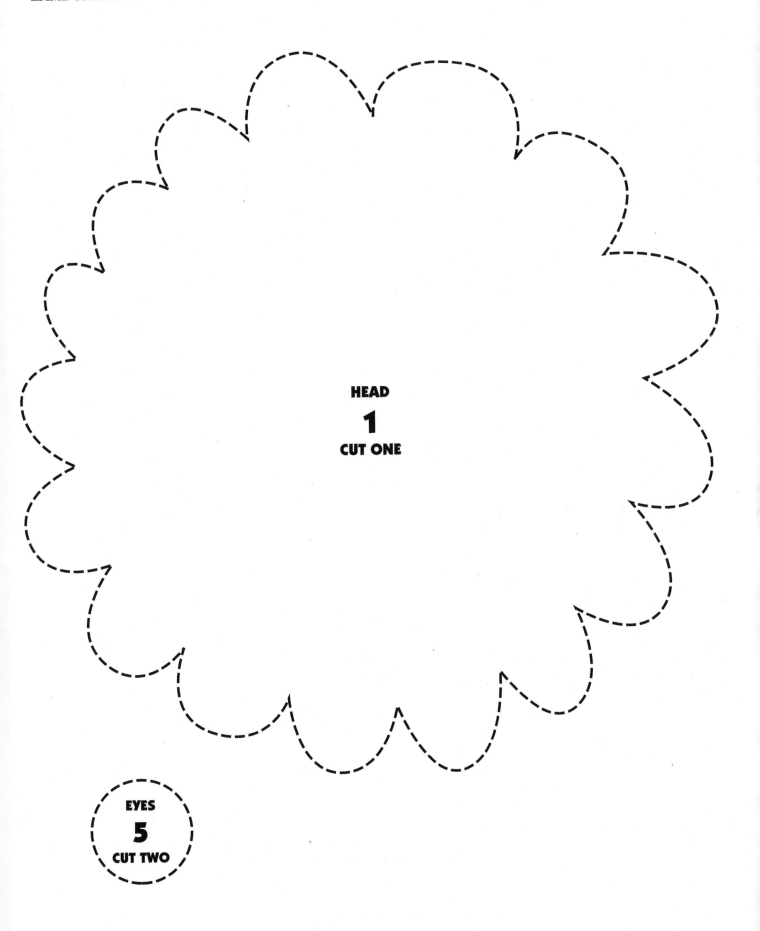

HEAD

1

CUT ONE

EYES

5

CUT TWO

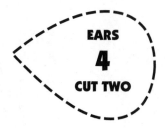

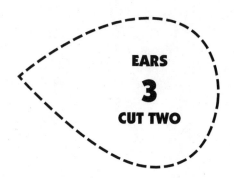

FACE

2

CUT ONE

Note:
This is how the lamb's mouth is rendered.
Use this to trace or copy.

Materials: *brown, beige and black paper; scissors; glue; black crayon or marker*

HORSE

1 Cut one #1 head from brown paper. Cut one #2 "blaze" from beige paper. Glue the blaze to the head as shown.

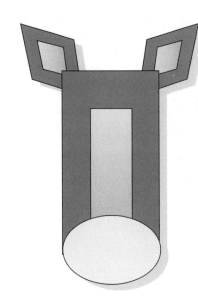

2 Cut one #3 muzzle from beige paper. Glue it to the bottom of the head as shown. Cut two #4 ears from brown paper. Cut two #5 ears from beige paper. Glue the #5 ears, centered, to the #4 ears. Glue the ears to the underside of the horse's head as shown.

3 Cut one #6 mane from beige paper. Glue it to the top of the horse's head. Cut two #7 eyes from black paper. Glue them to the head as shown.

4 Cut two #8 nostrils from black paper. Glue them to the muzzle as shown. Add a smile with black crayon or marker.

EYES
7
CUT TWO

NOSTRILS

8

CUT TWO

HEAD
1
CUT ONE

HORSE PATTERNS

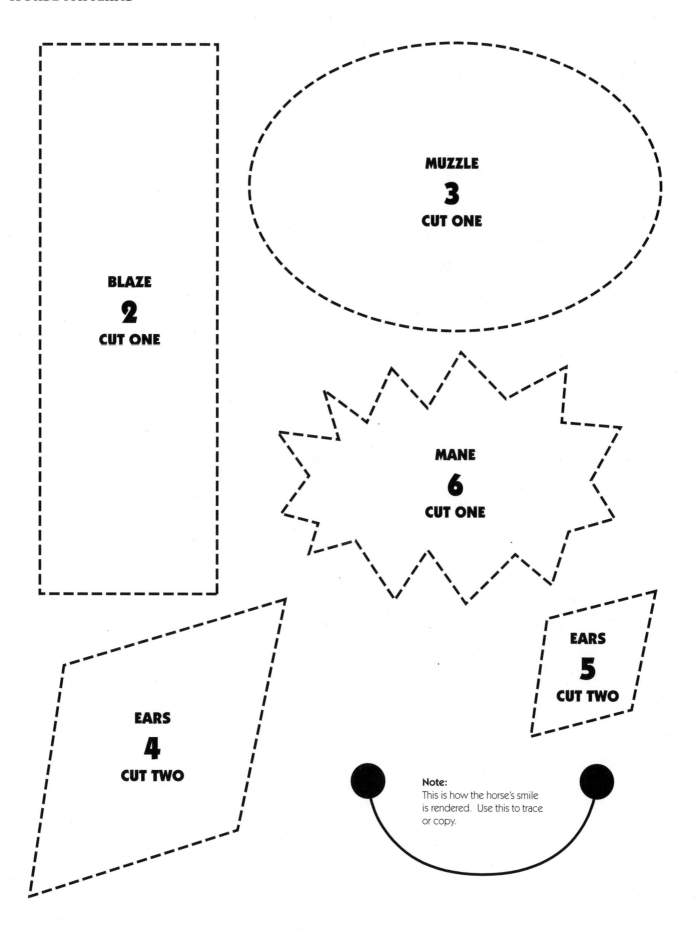

Materials: gray and black paper, scissors, glue, yarn

MOUSE

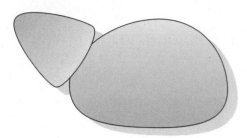

1 Cut one #1 body from gray paper. Cut one #2 head from gray paper. Glue the head to the body as shown.

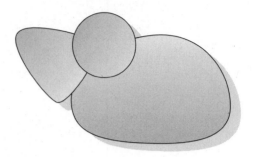

2 Cut two #3 ears from gray paper. Glue one to the mouse as shown.

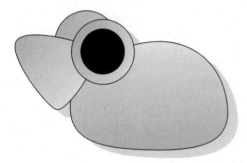

3 Glue the other #3 ear to the underside of the mouse as shown. Cut one #4 ear from black paper. Glue it, centered, to the #3 ear.

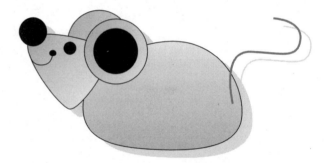

4 Cut one #5 nose from black paper. Glue it to the mouse's head as shown. Cut a piece of yarn and glue it to the back of the mouse as shown. With a black marker or crayon, add an eye and a smile.

MOUSE PATTERNS

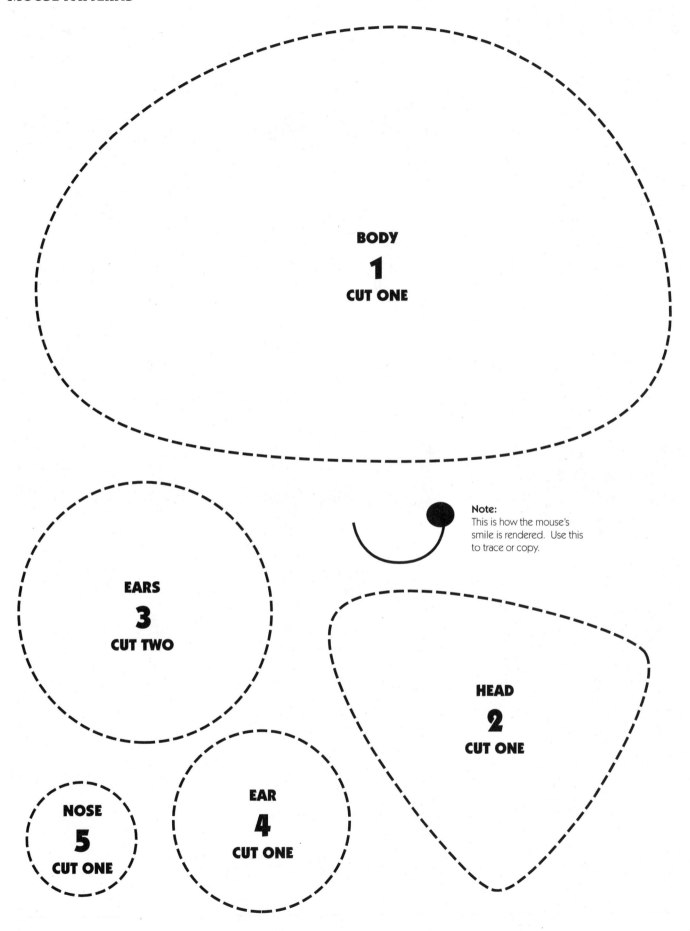

BODY
1
CUT ONE

Note:
This is how the mouse's smile is rendered. Use this to trace or copy.

EARS
3
CUT TWO

HEAD
2
CUT ONE

NOSE
5
CUT ONE

EAR
4
CUT ONE

RACCOON

1 Cut one #1 head from gray paper.

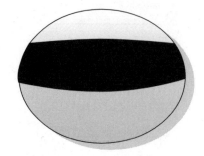

2 Cut one #2 mask from black paper. Glue it to the head as shown.

3 Cut two #3 eyes from white paper. Glue them to the mask. Cut two #4 ears from gray paper. Glue them to the head as shown.

4 Cut two #5 ears from black paper. Glue them, centered, to the #4 ears. Glue the ears to the raccoon's head as shown. Cut one #6 nose from gray paper. Glue it to the center of the raccoon's head.

5 Cut one #7 nose from black paper. Glue it to the bottom of the #6 nose.

6 Using a black crayon or marker, add eyes and a big smile to your raccoon.

RACCOON PATTERNS

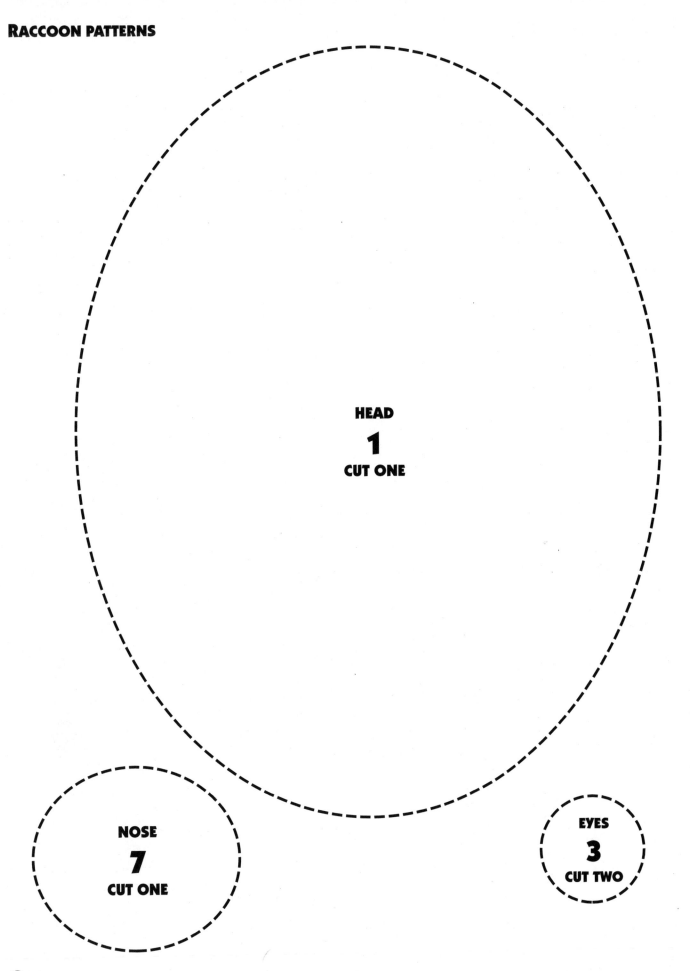

HEAD
1
CUT ONE

NOSE
7
CUT ONE

EYES
3
CUT TWO

RACCOON PATTERNS

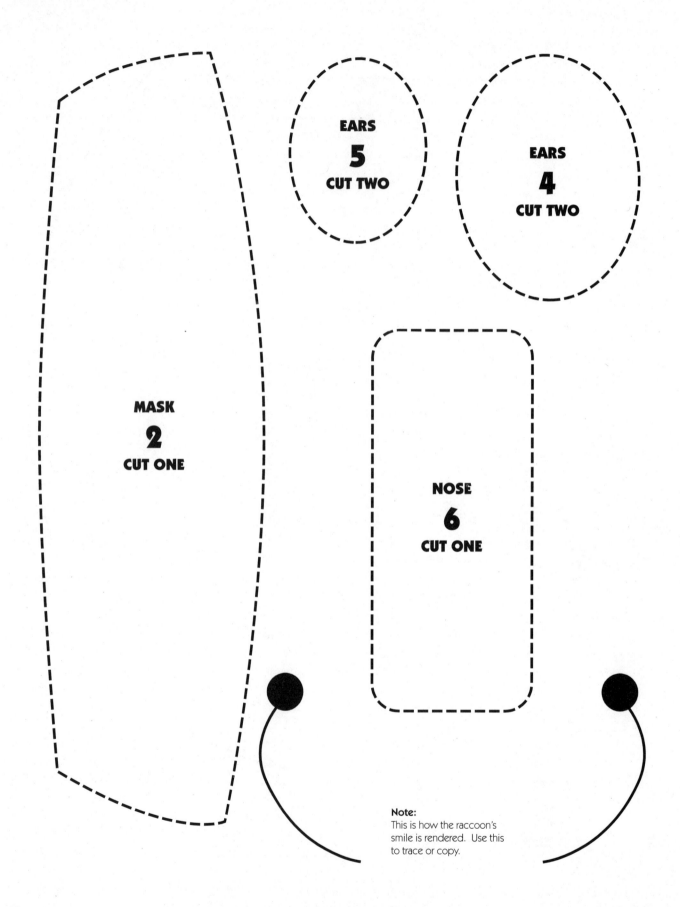

EARS
5
CUT TWO

EARS
4
CUT TWO

MASK
2
CUT ONE

NOSE
6
CUT ONE

Note:
This is how the raccoon's smile is rendered. Use this to trace or copy.

Materials: brown, yellow and red paper; scissors; glue; black marker or crayon

ROOSTER

1 Cut one #1 body from brown paper. Cut one #2 tail from brown paper. Glue the #2 tail to the body as shown.

2 Cut one #3 head from brown paper. Glue the head to the body.

3 Cut one #4 comb from red paper. Glue it to the underside of the rooster's head as shown.

4 Cut one #5 wattle from red paper. Glue it to the underside of the rooster's head. Cut one #6 leg from red paper. Glue it to the underside of the rooster's body as shown.

5 Cut one #7 beak from yellow paper. Glue it to the underside of the head as shown.

6 With a black marker or crayon, draw an eye and a smile on your rooster.

ROOSTER PATTERNS

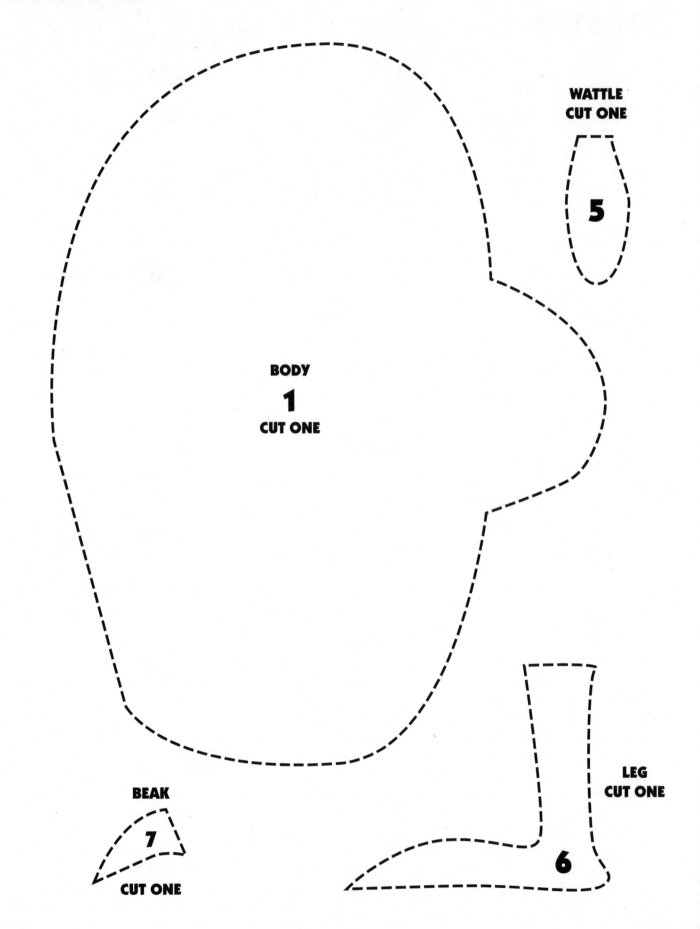

**WATTLE
CUT ONE**

5

**BODY

1

CUT ONE**

**LEG
CUT ONE**

6

BEAK

7

CUT ONE

ROOSTER PATTERNS

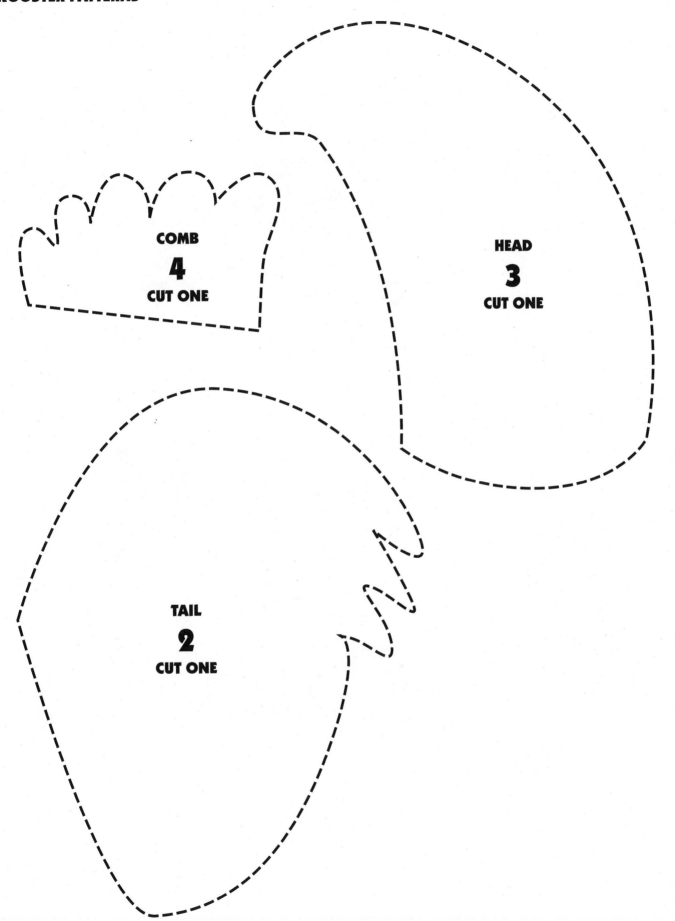

COMB
4
CUT ONE

HEAD
3
CUT ONE

TAIL
2
CUT ONE

HEN

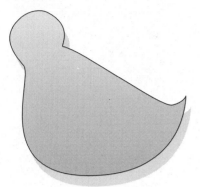

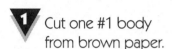

▼ **1** Cut one #1 body from brown paper.

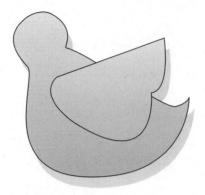

▼ **2** Cut one #2 wing from brown paper. Glue it to the body as shown.

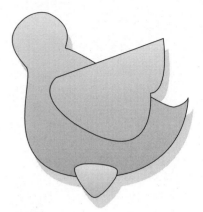

▼ **3** Cut one #3 thigh from brown paper. Glue it to the bottom of the #1 body.

▼ **4** Cut one #4 beak from yellow paper. Glue it to the underside of the hen's head. Cut one #5 leg from red paper. Glue it to the underside of the thigh as shown.

▼ **5** Cut two #6 pattern pieces. Glue one to the underside of the top of the head. Glue the other to the underside of the bottom of the hen's head.

▼ **6** With a black crayon or marker, add an eye and a smile to your happy hen!

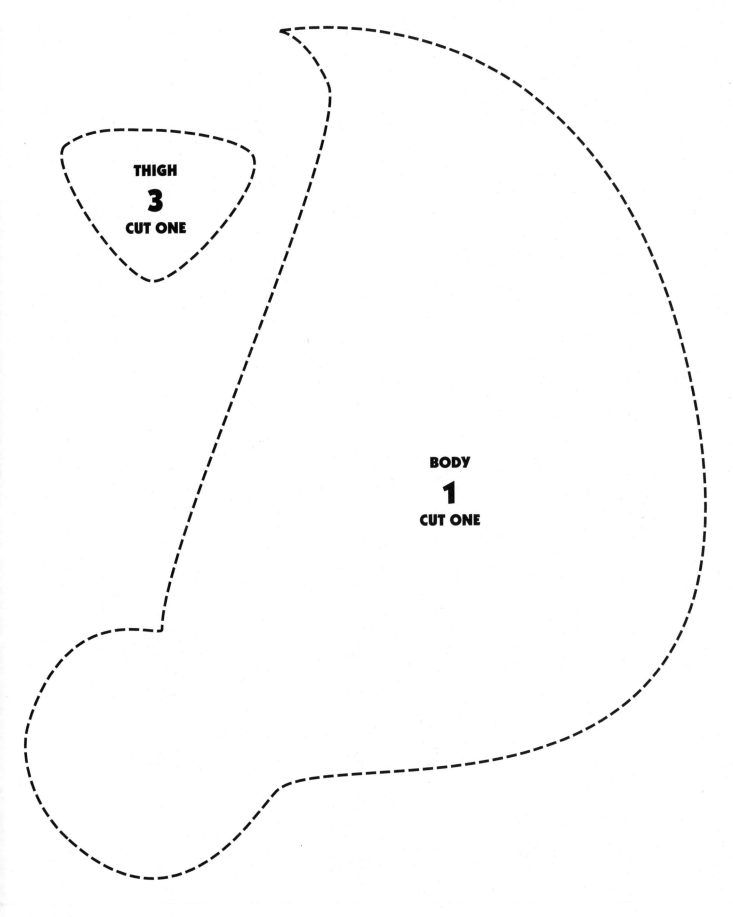

THIGH
3
CUT ONE

BODY
1
CUT ONE

HEN PATTERNS

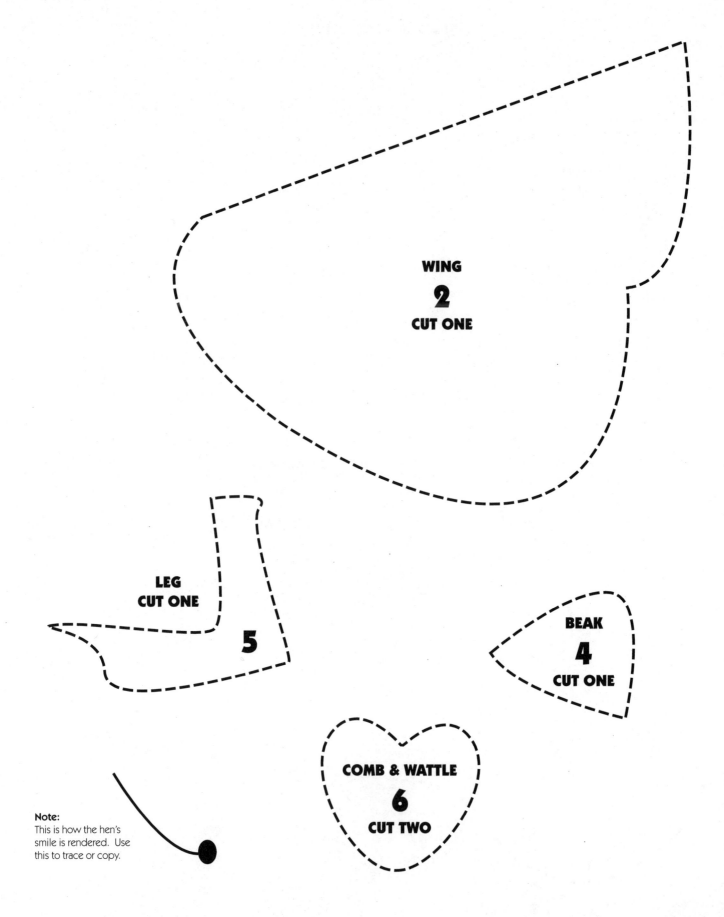

WING
2
CUT ONE

LEG
CUT ONE
5

BEAK
4
CUT ONE

COMB & WATTLE
6
CUT TWO

Note:
This is how the hen's
smile is rendered. Use
this to trace or copy.

CHICK

CHICK

1 Cut one #1 body from yellow paper.

2 Cut one #2 head from yellow paper. Glue it to the #1 body as shown.

3 Cut one #3 shell from white paper. Glue it to the body as shown.

4 Cut one #4 shell from white paper. Glue it to the #3 shell as shown.

5 Cut one #5 beak from orange paper. Glue it to the chick's head. Cut one #6 eye from white paper. Glue it to the chick's head as shown.

6 Using scissors, make several small cuts along the back of the chick's head to represent "down." With a black crayon or marker, add an eye and a smile to your chick.

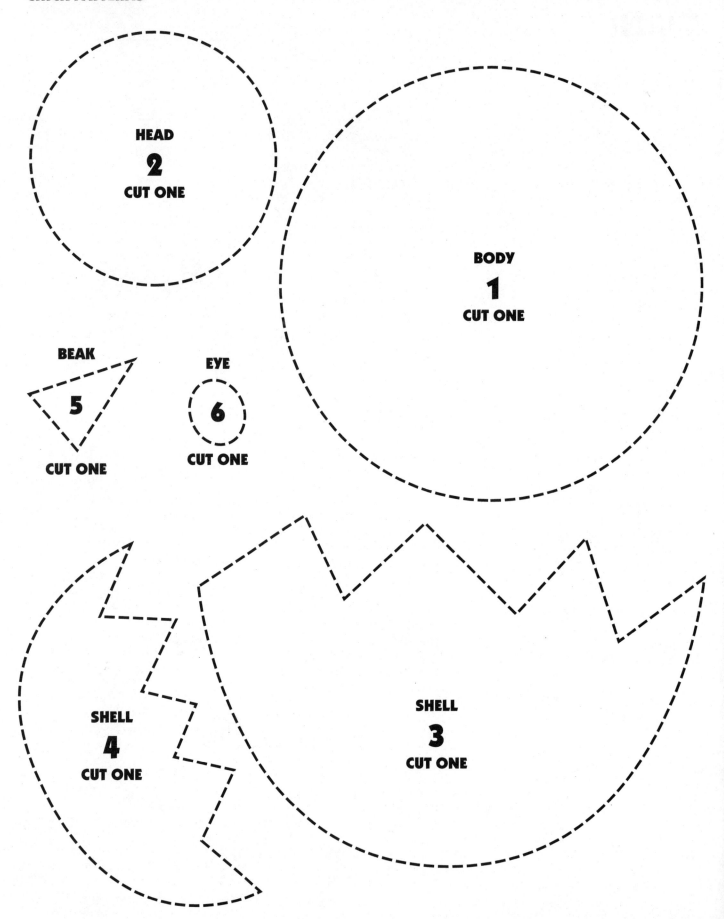

Materials: *brown, beige, orange, yellow and white paper;*
scissors; glue; black crayon or marker

Duck

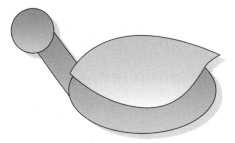

1 Cut one #1 body from brown paper. Cut one #2 neck from brown paper. Glue the body to the neck as shown.

2 Cut one #3 head from brown paper. Glue it to the neck as shown.

3 Cut one #4 wing from beige paper. Glue it to the duck's body.

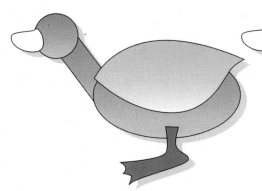

4 Cut one #5 bill from yellow paper. Glue it to the duck's head as shown. Cut two #6 legs from orange paper. Glue one to the duck's body as shown.

5 Glue the other leg to the underside of the duck's body as shown.

6 Cut one #7 eye from white paper. Glue it to the duck's head as shown. With a black crayon or marker, add another oval to the eye and a smile to your duck.

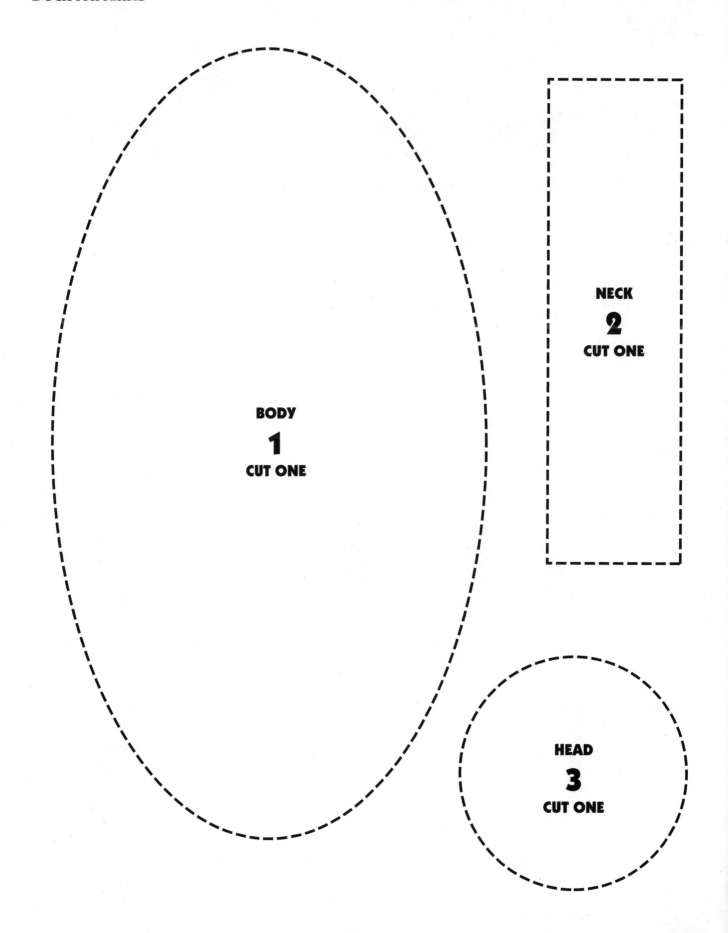

NECK
2
CUT ONE

BODY
1
CUT ONE

HEAD
3
CUT ONE

DUCK PATTERNS

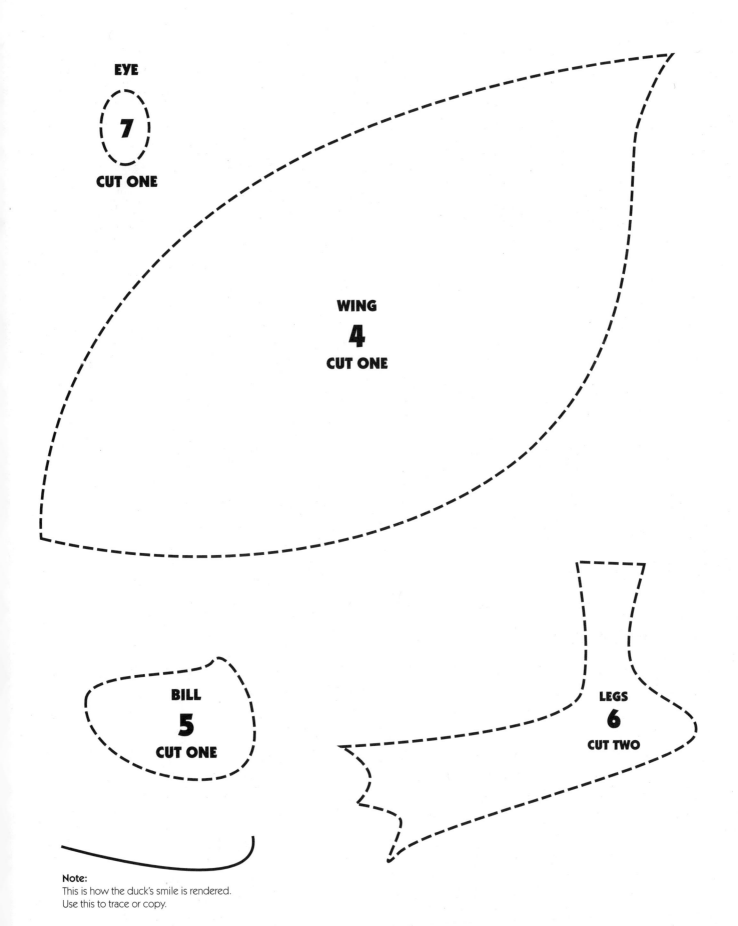

EYE

7

CUT ONE

WING

4

CUT ONE

BILL

5

CUT ONE

LEGS

6

CUT TWO

Note:
This is how the duck's smile is rendered.
Use this to trace or copy.

Materials: *yellow, orange, brown, white and black paper; scissors; glue; black marker or crayon*

CAT

 Cut one #1 head from yellow paper.

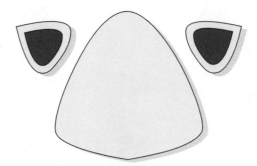

 Cut two #2 ears from yellow paper. Cut two #3 ears from brown paper. Glue the #3 ears, centered, to the #2 ears.

3 Cut two #4 muzzles from yellow paper. Glue the muzzles to the cat's face as shown. Glue the ears to the underside of the cat's head.

4 Cut one #5 nose from brown paper. Glue it to the top of the muzzles.

5 Cut two #6 eyes from white paper. Glue them onto the cat's face above the nose. Cut two #7 eyes from black paper. Glue them to the #6 eyes as shown.

6 Cut two of each of the #8 stripes. Glue them, as shown, to the cat's face. Make small cuts along the bottom of the cat's face as shown. With a black crayon or marker, add a smile to the cat.

CAT PATTERNS

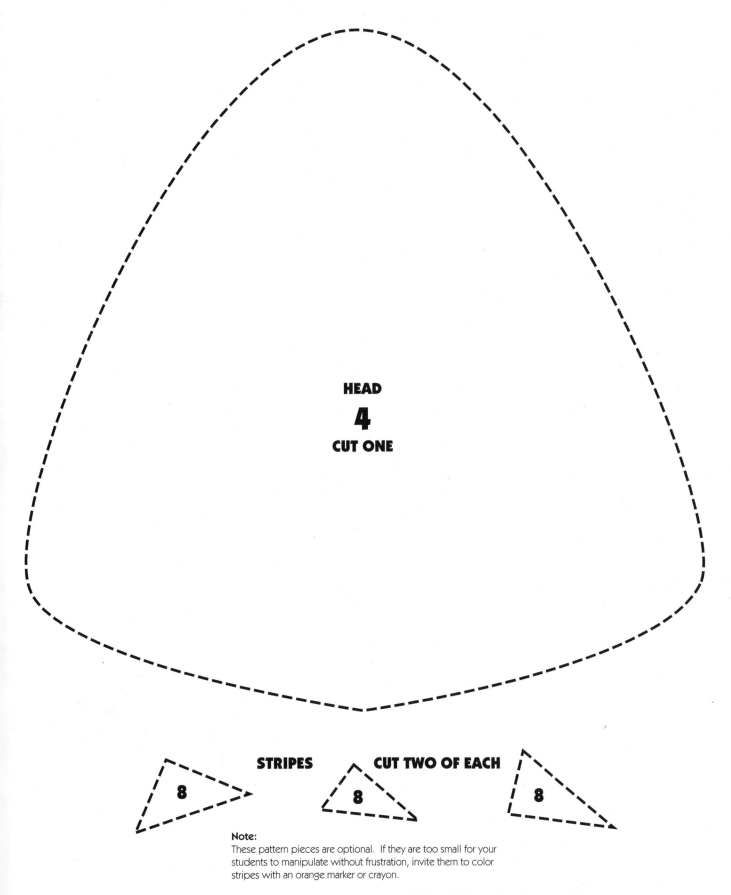

HEAD

4

CUT ONE

STRIPES   **CUT TWO OF EACH**

8   8   8

Note:
These pattern pieces are optional. If they are too small for your students to manipulate without frustration, invite them to color stripes with an orange marker or crayon.

CAT PATTERNS

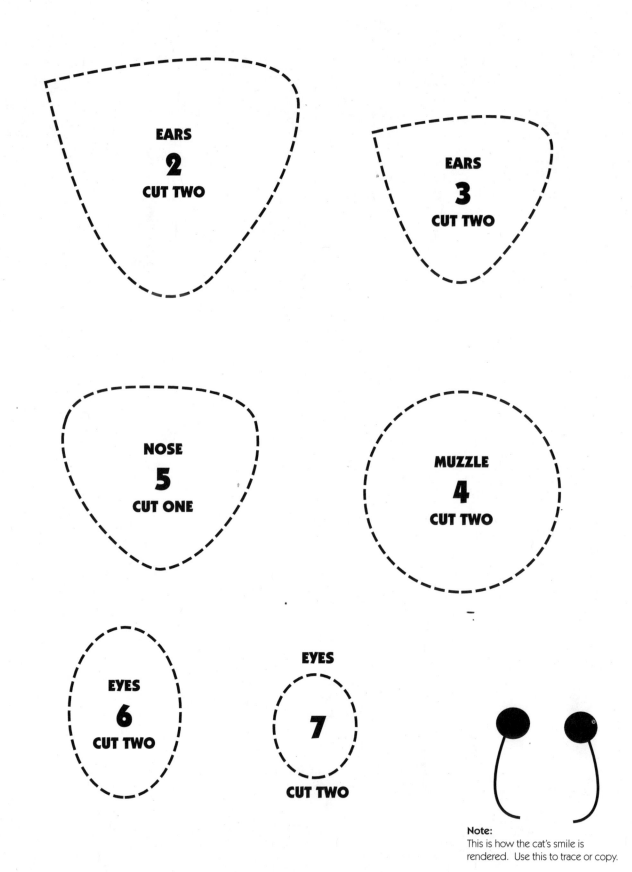

EARS
2
CUT TWO

EARS
3
CUT TWO

NOSE
5
CUT ONE

MUZZLE
4
CUT TWO

EYES
6
CUT TWO

EYES
7
CUT TWO

Note:
This is how the cat's smile is rendered. Use this to trace or copy.

DOG

Materials: *white, black and brown paper; scissors; glue; black marker or crayon*

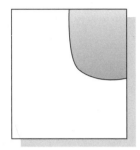

1 Cut one #1 head from white paper. Cut one #2 spot from brown paper. Glue the brown spot to the upper right corner of the dog's face.

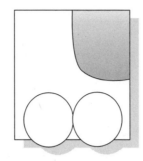

2 Cut two #3 muzzles from white paper. Glue them to the face as shown.

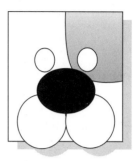

3 Cut one #4 nose from black paper. Glue it to the dog's face, overlapping the muzzle as shown. Cut two #5 eyes from white paper. Glue them to the face as shown.

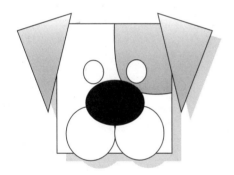

4 Cut two #6 ears from brown paper. Glue them to the dog's head as shown.

5 Cut one #7 "tuft" from brown paper. Glue it to the underside of the dog's head as shown.

6 Cut two #8 eyes from black paper. Glue them to the #5 eyes as shown. With a black crayon or marker, add some freckles and a smile to your loyal ol' farm dog.

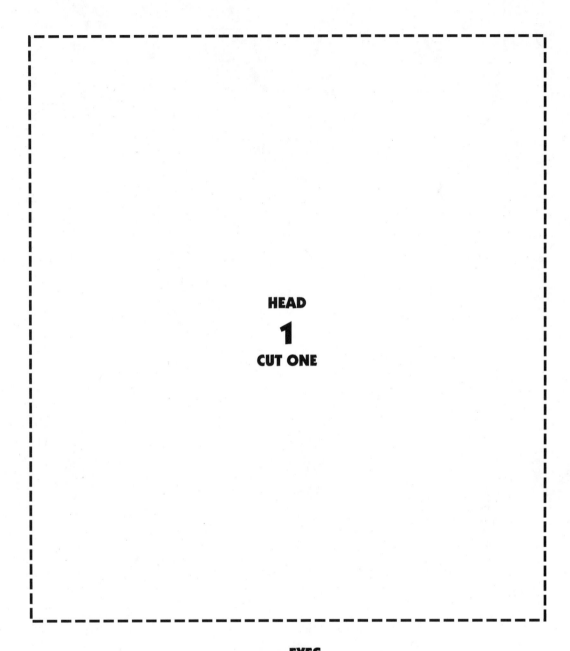

HEAD

1

CUT ONE

EYES

5

CUT TWO

EYES

8

CUT TWO

Note:
This pattern piece is optional. If it is too small for your students to manipulate without frustration, invite them to color the eyes in with a black crayon or marker.

TUFT

7

CUT ONE

DOG PATTERNS

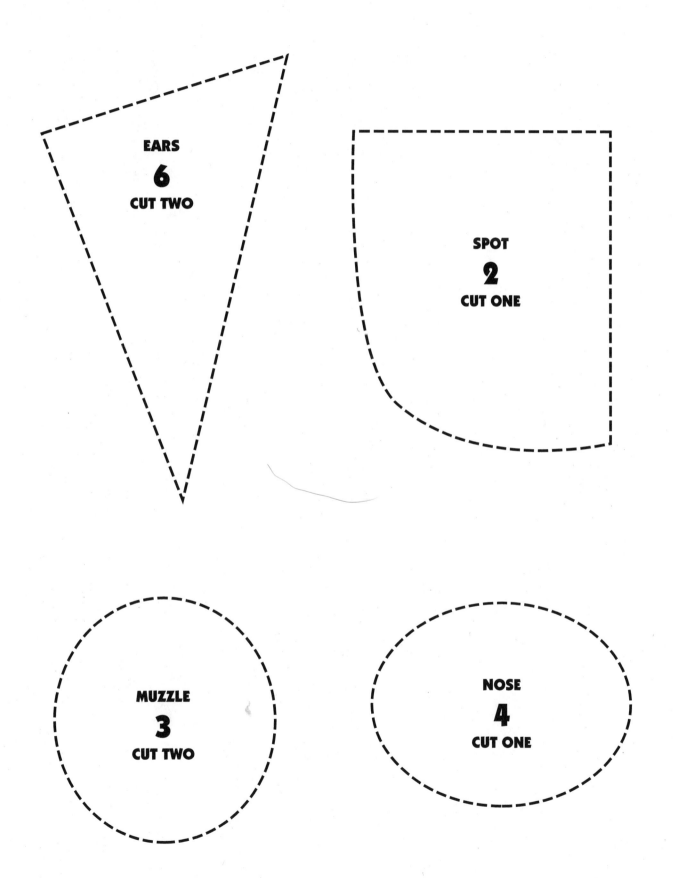

EARS
6
CUT TWO

SPOT
2
CUT ONE

MUZZLE
3
CUT TWO

NOSE
4
CUT ONE

Materials: *red, brown, yellow, white and black paper; scissors; glue; black marker or crayon*

BARN

1 Cut one #1 barn from red paper. With a black crayon or marker, draw horizontal stripes on the barn.

2 Cut one #2 barn door from brown paper. Glue it to the #1 barn as shown. With a black crayon or marker, draw vertical stripes on the door.

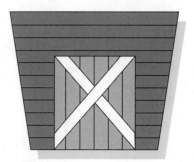

3 Cut two #3 door supports from white paper. Glue them, as shown to the barn door.

4 Cut one #4 barn roof from white paper. Glue it to the top of the barn as shown.

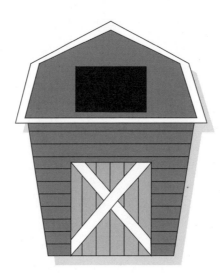

5 Cut one #5 barn roof from red paper. Glue it, centered, to the #4 barn roof. Cut one #6 hayloft from black paper. Glue it to the red barn roof as shown.

6 Cut one #7 hay pattern piece from yellow paper. Glue it to the hayloft.

BARN PATTERNS

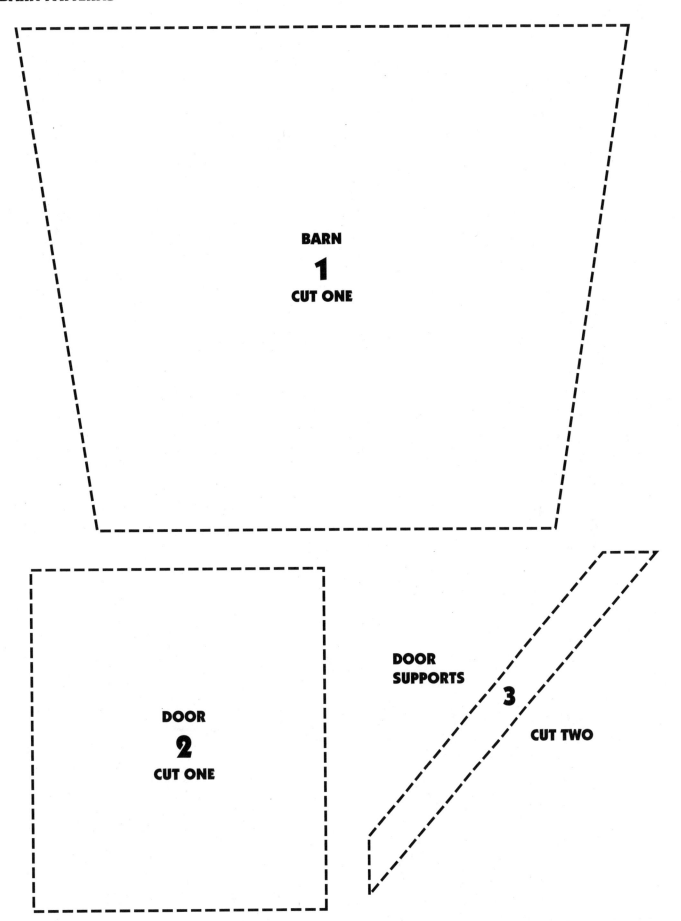

BARN

1

CUT ONE

DOOR

2

CUT ONE

DOOR SUPPORTS

3

CUT TWO

BARN PATTERNS

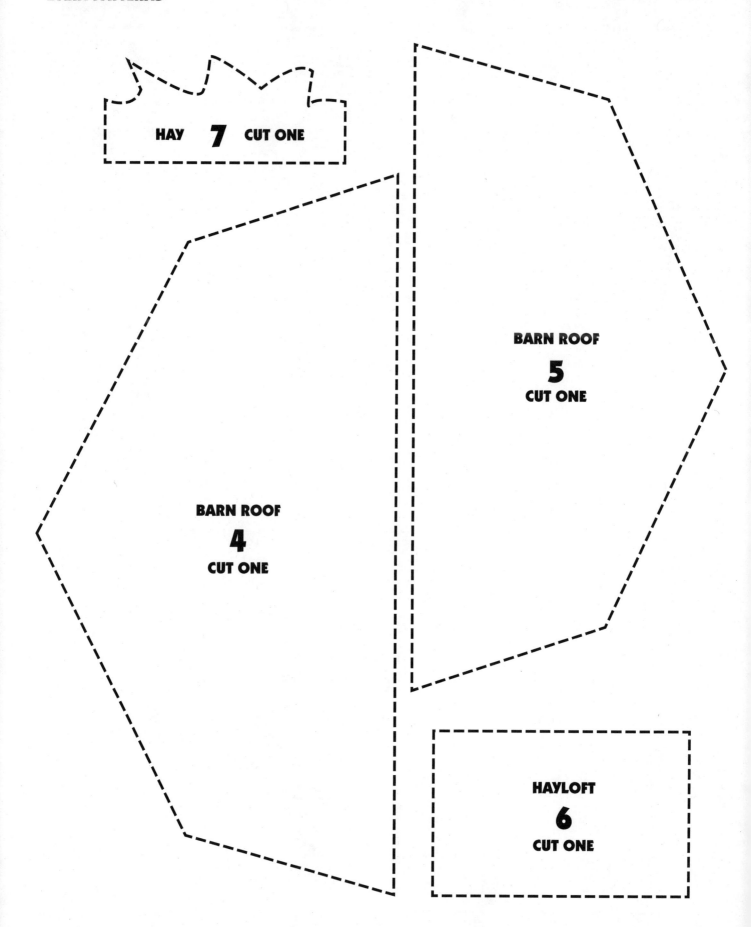

HAY **7** CUT ONE

BARN ROOF **5** CUT ONE

BARN ROOF **4** CUT ONE

HAYLOFT **6** CUT ONE

Materials: red, white, gray and black paper; scissors; glue

SILO

1 Cut one #1 silo from red paper.

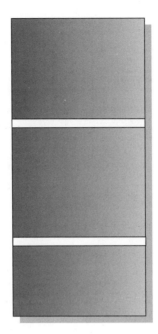

2 Cut two #2 stripes from white paper. Glue them, as shown, to the silo.

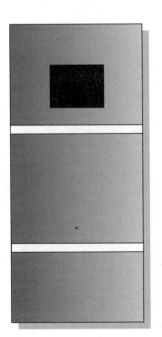

3 Cut one #3 window from black paper. Glue it, centered, to the top third of the silo.

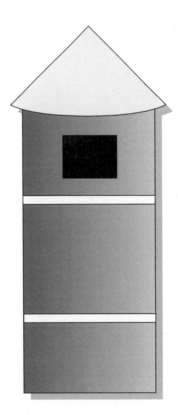

4 Cut one #4 roof from gray paper. Glue it to the top of the silo.

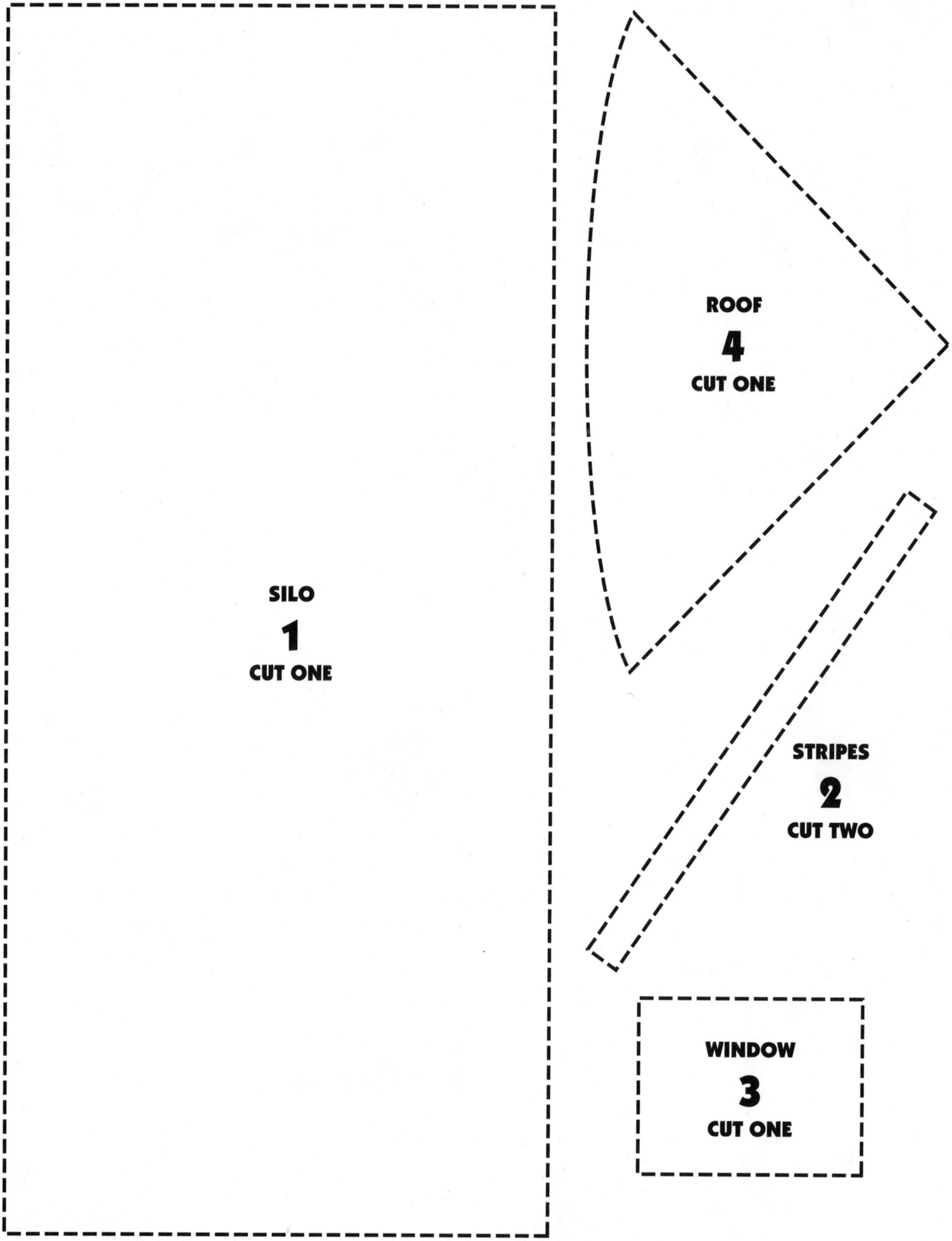

SILO PATTERNS

SILO

1

CUT ONE

ROOF

4

CUT ONE

STRIPES

2

CUT TWO

WINDOW

3

CUT ONE

FARM HOUSE

Materials: white, blue, red and gray paper; scissors; glue; black crayon or marker

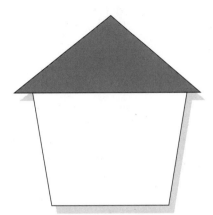

1 Cut one #1 house from white paper. Cut one #2 roof from blue paper. Glue the roof to the housetop.

2 Cut one #3 roof from white paper. Glue it to the #2 roof. Cut one #4 door from red paper. Glue it to the house.

3 With a black crayon or marker, draw horizontal stripes on the white roof. Cut two #5 windows and two #6 windows. Glue them to the house as shown.

4 Cut one #7 window from gray paper. Glue it to the roof. Cut one #8 door glass from gray paper. Glue it to the red door. Cut four #9 shutters from red paper. Glue them on either side of each #6 window as shown.

5 Cut one #10 chimney from red paper. Glue it to the underside of the roof as shown. With a black marker or crayon, add horizontal stripes to the shutters and a few rectangles to the chimney.

6 With a black marker or crayon, add a doorknob and vertical and horizontal lines to each rectangular window.

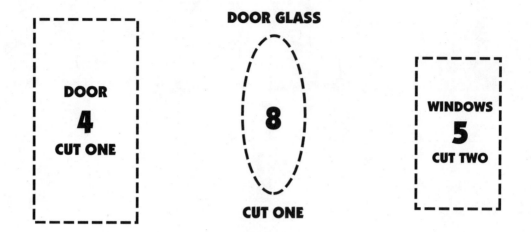

DOOR GLASS

DOOR
4
CUT ONE

8

CUT ONE

WINDOWS
5
CUT TWO

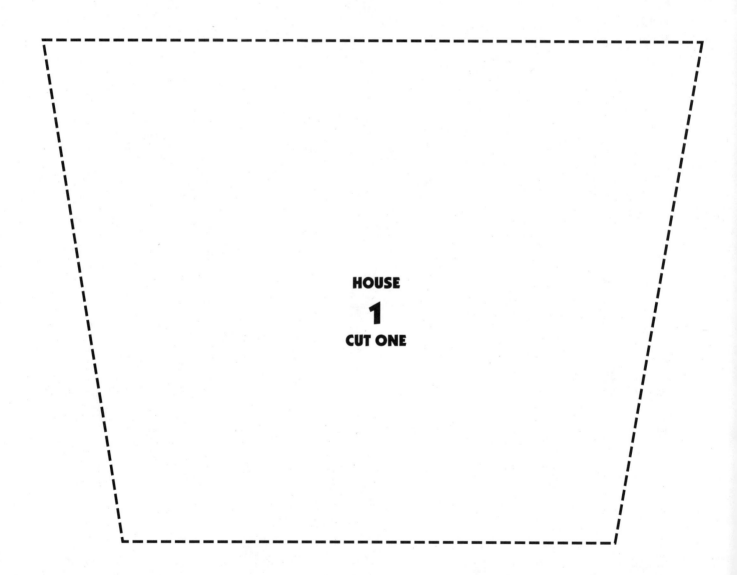

HOUSE
1
CUT ONE

FARM HOUSE PATTERNS

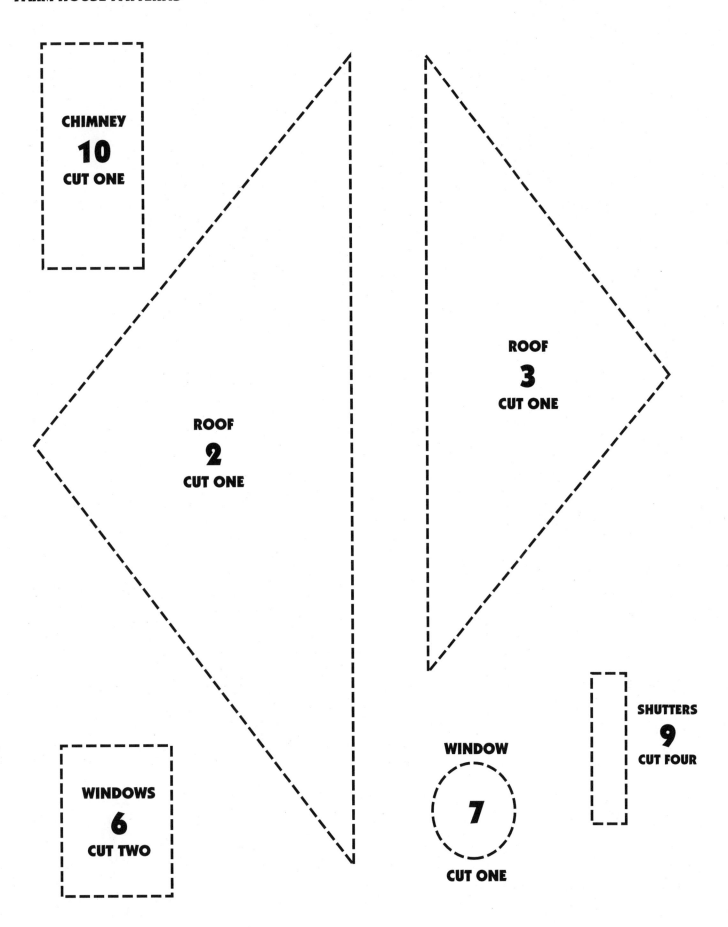

CHIMNEY
10
CUT ONE

ROOF
2
CUT ONE

ROOF
3
CUT ONE

WINDOWS
6
CUT TWO

WINDOW
7
CUT ONE

SHUTTERS
9
CUT FOUR

Materials: red and black paper, scissors, glue, black crayon or marker

HENHOUSE

1 Cut one #1 top from red paper. Cut one #2 bottom from red paper. Glue the top to the bottom.

2 Cut three #3 windows from black paper. Glue them, in a row, to the lower half of the #1 top.

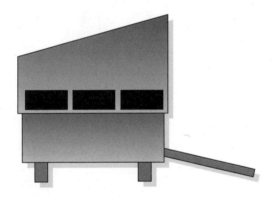

3 Cut two #4 legs from red paper. Glue them to the underside of the henhouse as shown. Cut one #5 ramp from red paper. Glue it to the henhouse as shown.

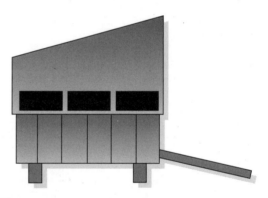

4 With a black crayon or marker, draw vertical stripes on the bottom half of the henhouse.

HENHOUSE PATTERNS

TOP

1

CUT ONE

WINDOWS

3

CUT THREE

LEGS

4

CUT TWO

RAMP

5

CUT ONE

BOTTOM

2

CUT ONE

Materials: *brown paper, scissors, glue*

GATE

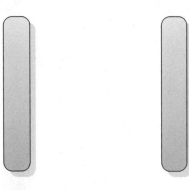

1 Cut two #1 fence posts from brown paper. Lay them on a tabletop as shown.

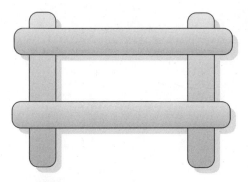

2 Cut two #2 horizontal slats from brown paper. Glue them, as shown, to the fence posts.

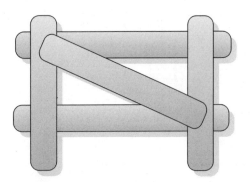

3 Cut two #3 crossbars from brown paper. Glue the first one, as shown, to the gate.

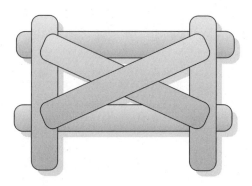

4 Glue the second crossbar to the gate as shown.

GATE PATTERNS

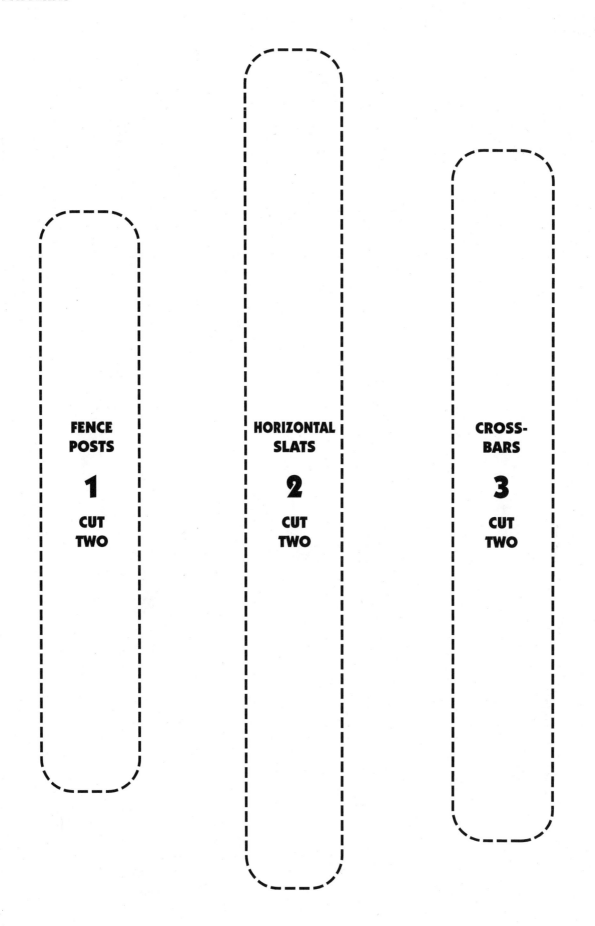

FENCE
POSTS

1

CUT
TWO

HORIZONTAL
SLATS

2

CUT
TWO

CROSS-
BARS

3

CUT
TWO

Materials: *green, black and yellow paper; scissors; glue; black crayon or marker*

TRACTOR

1 Cut one #1 frame from green paper. Cut one #2 motor housing from green paper. Glue the motor housing to the frame as shown.

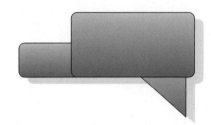

2 Cut one #3 front axle from green paper. Glue it to the underside of the tractor as shown.

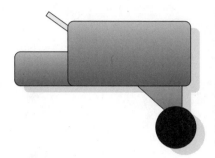

3 Cut one #4 wheel from black paper. Glue it to the front axle. Cut one #5 steering column from green paper. Glue it to the motor housing as shown.

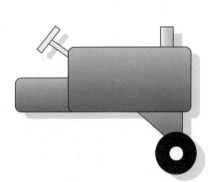

4 Cut one #6 steering wheel from green paper. Glue it to the steering column. Cut one #7 muffler from green paper. Glue it to the underside of the top of the motor housing. Cut one #8 hubcap from yellow paper and glue it, centered, to the #4 wheel.

5 Cut one #9 wheel from black paper. Glue it to the #1 frame as shown. Cut one #10 muffler from green paper. Glue it to the underside of the #7 muffler.

6 Cut one #11 hubcap from yellow paper. Glue it to the center of the #9 wheel. Cut four #12 ventilation slats from black paper. Glue them to the front of the motor housing as shown.

TRACTOR PATTERNS

MOTOR HOUSING

2

CUT ONE

FRAME

1

CUT ONE

STEERING COLUMN

5

CUT ONE

6

STEERING WHEEL
CUT ONE

TRACTOR PATTERNS

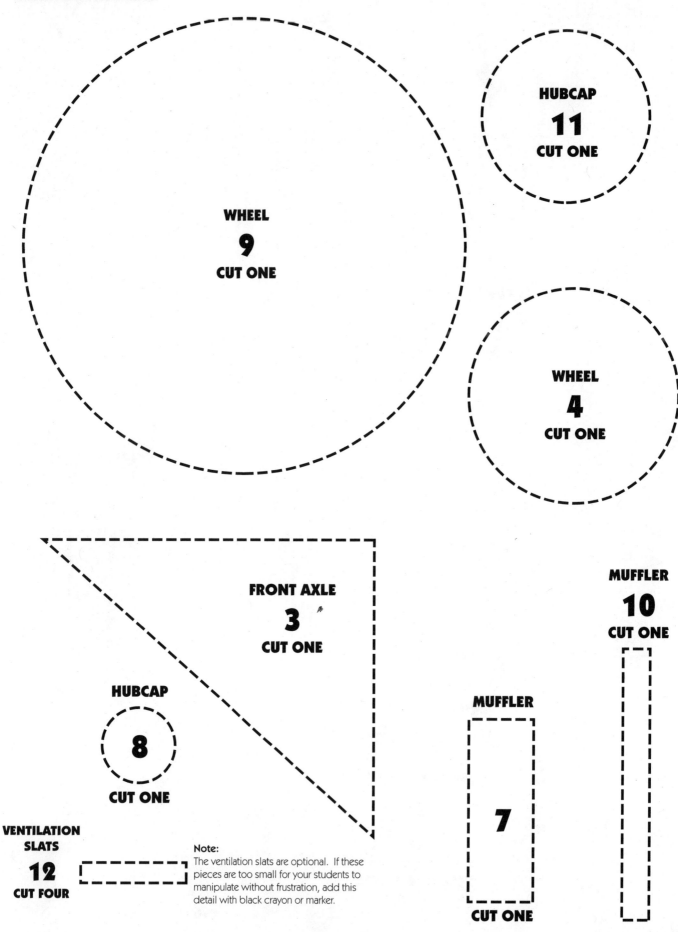

WHEEL
9
CUT ONE

HUBCAP
11
CUT ONE

WHEEL
4
CUT ONE

FRONT AXLE
3
CUT ONE

HUBCAP
8
CUT ONE

MUFFLER
10
CUT ONE

MUFFLER
7
CUT ONE

VENTILATION
SLATS
12
CUT FOUR

Note:
The ventilation slats are optional. If these pieces are too small for your students to manipulate without frustration, add this detail with black crayon or marker.

Materials: red, green, black and white paper; scissors; glue; black crayon or marker

FARM TRUCK

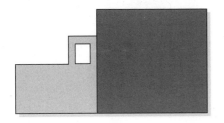

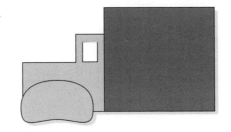

1 Cut one #1 truck bed from red paper. Cut one #2 truck from green paper. Glue the truck bed to the truck as shown. Cut one #3 window from white paper. Glue it to the truck as shown.

2 Cut one #4 wheel well from green paper. Glue it to the #2 truck.

3 Cut two #5 tires from black paper. Glue them to the bottom of the farm truck as shown.

4 Cut two #6 hubcaps from white paper. Glue them, centered, to the #5 tires.

5 With a black crayon or marker, add horizontal stripes to the truck bed.

6 Cut two #7 supports from white paper. One support will need to be trimmed slightly to accommodate the back wheel. Glue them to the truck bed as shown.

TRUCK BED

1

CUT ONE

SUPPORTS

7

CUT TWO

FARM TRUCK PATTERNS

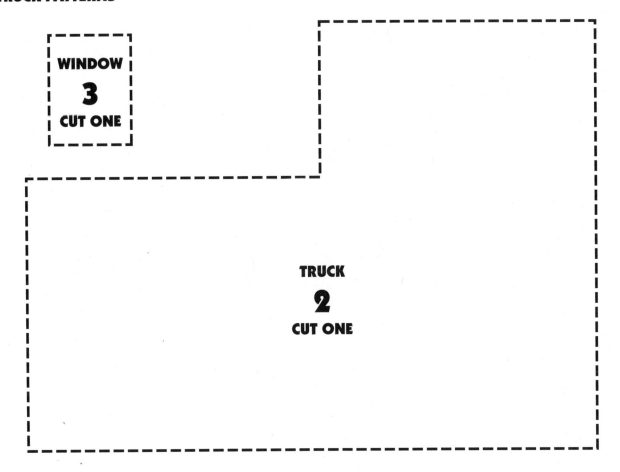

WINDOW
3
CUT ONE

TRUCK
2
CUT ONE

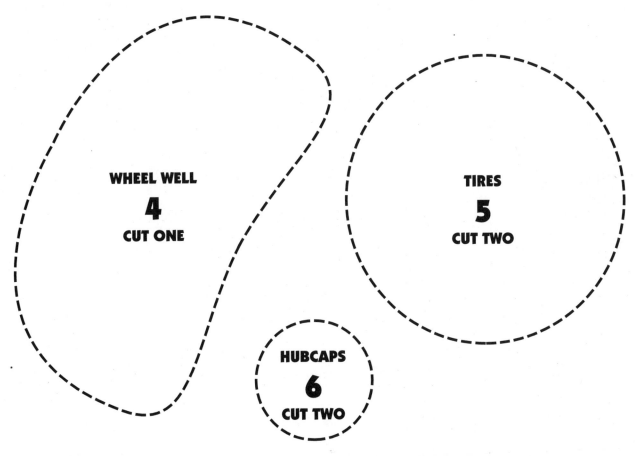

WHEEL WELL
4
CUT ONE

TIRES
5
CUT TWO

HUBCAPS
6
CUT TWO

Materials: *yellow, red and green paper; scissors; glue; black crayon or marker*

HARVEST BASKET

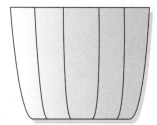

1 Cut one #1 basket from yellow paper. With a black crayon or marker, add vertical stripes to the basket.

2 Cut one #2 band and one #3 band, each from yellow paper. Glue them to the basket as shown.

3 Cut one #4 ear of corn from yellow paper. Cut two #5 corn husks from green paper. Glue them to the ear of corn as shown.

4 Glue the ear of corn to the underside of the harvest basket. Cut two #6 apples, one from red paper and one from green paper.

5 Glue the two apples to the underside of your harvest basket as shown.

6 With a black crayon or marker, create "kernels" on your ear of corn by drawing several horizontal and vertical lines.

HARVEST BASKET PATTERNS

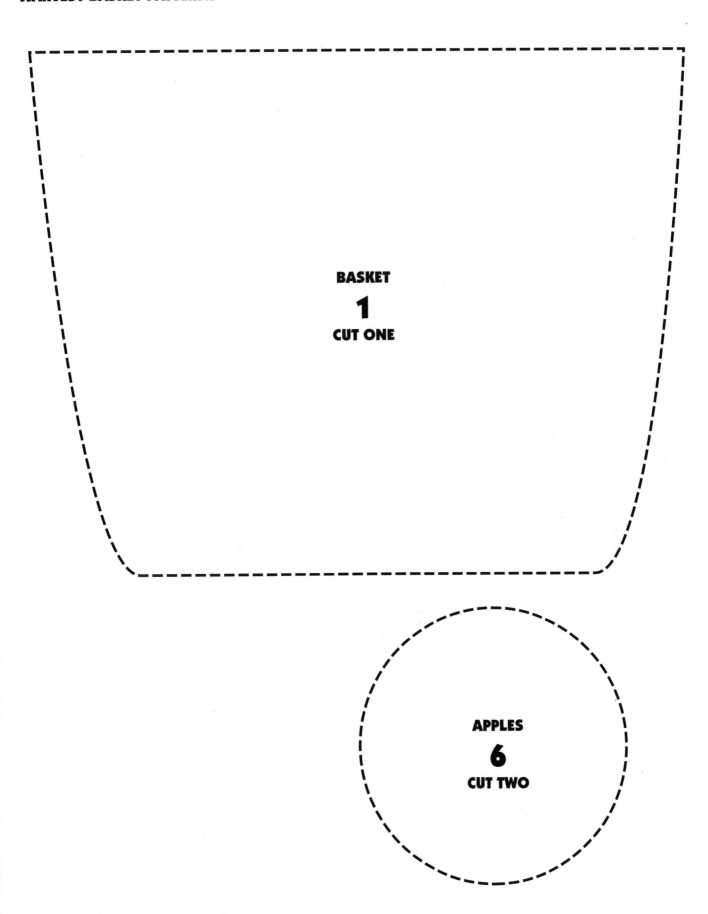

BASKET

1

CUT ONE

APPLES

6

CUT TWO

HARVEST BASKET PATTERNS

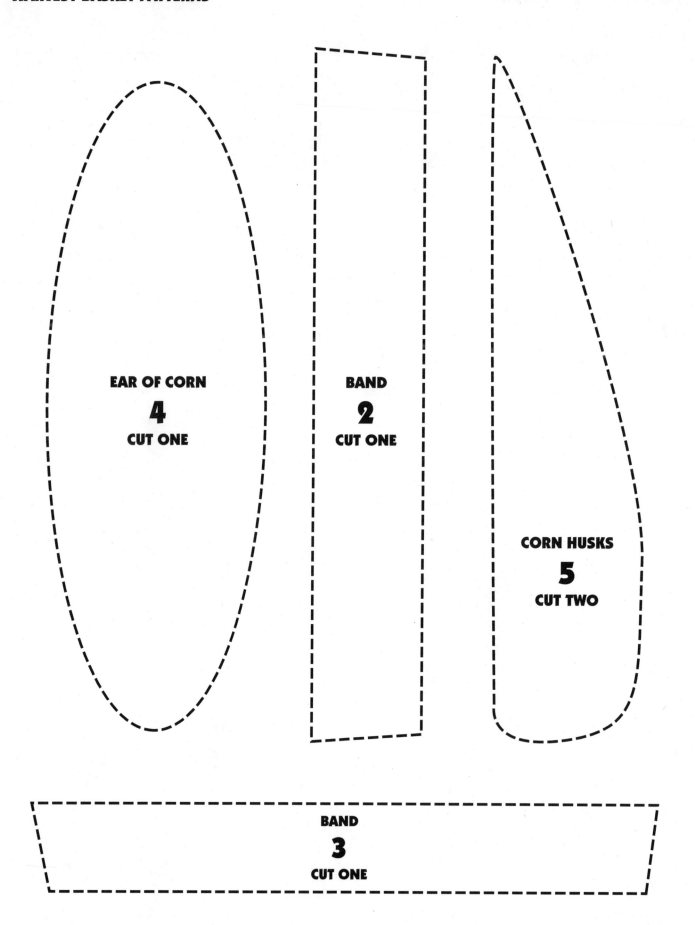

EAR OF CORN
4
CUT ONE

BAND
2
CUT ONE

CORN HUSKS
5
CUT TWO

BAND
3
CUT ONE

HARVEST BASKET PATTERNS

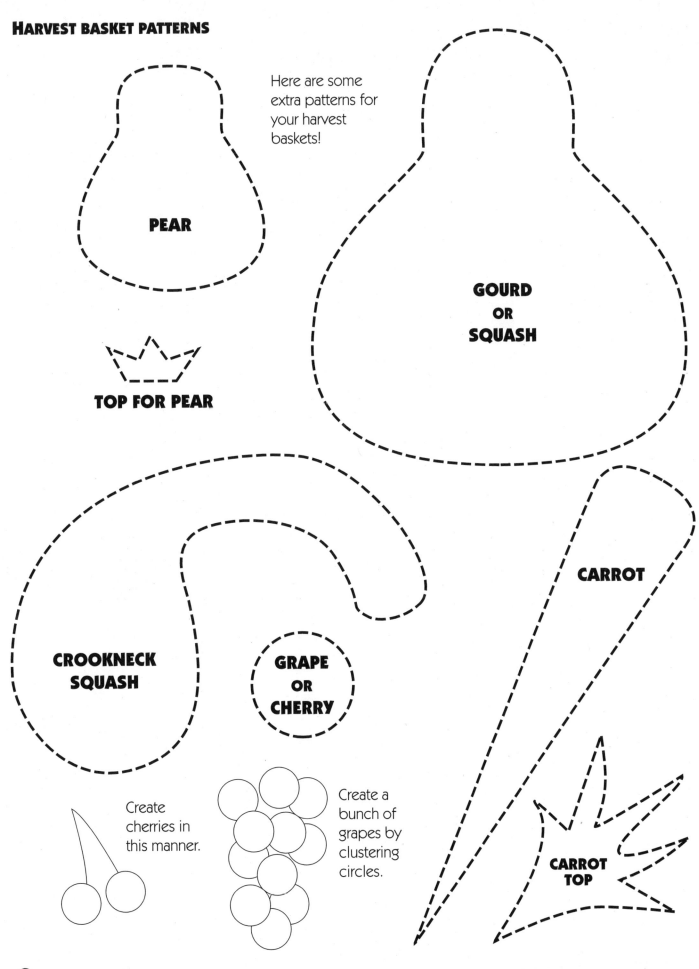

Here are some extra patterns for your harvest baskets!

PEAR

TOP FOR PEAR

GOURD OR SQUASH

CROOKNECK SQUASH

GRAPE OR CHERRY

CARROT

Create cherries in this manner.

Create a bunch of grapes by clustering circles.

CARROT TOP

SUGGESTIONS FOR USING PATTERNS

OPTION 1

Cut one of each pattern piece. Trace the pieces onto poster board, or any other paper you have that is sturdy, yet thin enough to cut with scissors. Transcribe the information printed on each pattern piece to the poster board pieces. Make as many sets of these as you predict you will need for your groups of students. Invite your students to trace around these pieces onto the appropriate color of paper. You will also need to photocopy the directions page for each Cut and Create farm pattern. Your students can use this for a visual, step-by-step guide to help them "build" their project. Laminate the directions page to add to their life span. Make as many photocopies of the directions page as you have sets of pattern pieces. Store each set in a Ziploc™ bag.

OPTION 2

Here's a quick and easy suggestion. Use this method when you're in a hurry and preparing a Cut and Create activity for only one or two students. First, tape the pattern page(s) up to a window or light box. Hold the appropriate color of paper up to the pattern page and trace the pattern piece, piece number and then indicate how many pieces the student will need to cut of each piece. Both this method and Option 1 allow you to edit out any pieces you feel are too small for your students to successfully manipulate. Photocopy a directions page for each student. Provide students with your tracings, a directions page and the materials listed and they will have everything they need to do their project.

OPTION 3

Photocopy the patterns directly onto 8½" x 11" (21.59 x 27.94 cm) colored paper. This will involve some cutting and pasting. Cut apart the pattern page(s) and glue the pattern pieces to be cut from a single color onto one sheet of white paper. Photocopy a set of these pattern pages for each student. You will also need to make several photocopies of the directions page, one for each group of students.

Note: Laminate your students' Cut and Create projects. Use a staple gun to staple them to a paint stick and put them in your drama corner, prop box or next to an appropriate story in your classroom library. Your students will love to role-play and dialogue with their farm animals!

PATTERNS FOR A CUT AND CREATE FARM

Here are some additional ideas to help you create a farm scene on a wall or bulletin board.

A sun can be created with a circle and some strips of yellow paper. Add eyes, a nose and a smile.

Make a rain cloud from gray or blue paper. Tinsel would make nice rain.

Surround your pond with cattails made from these simple shapes.

A wide, irregular blue blob will make a great pond.

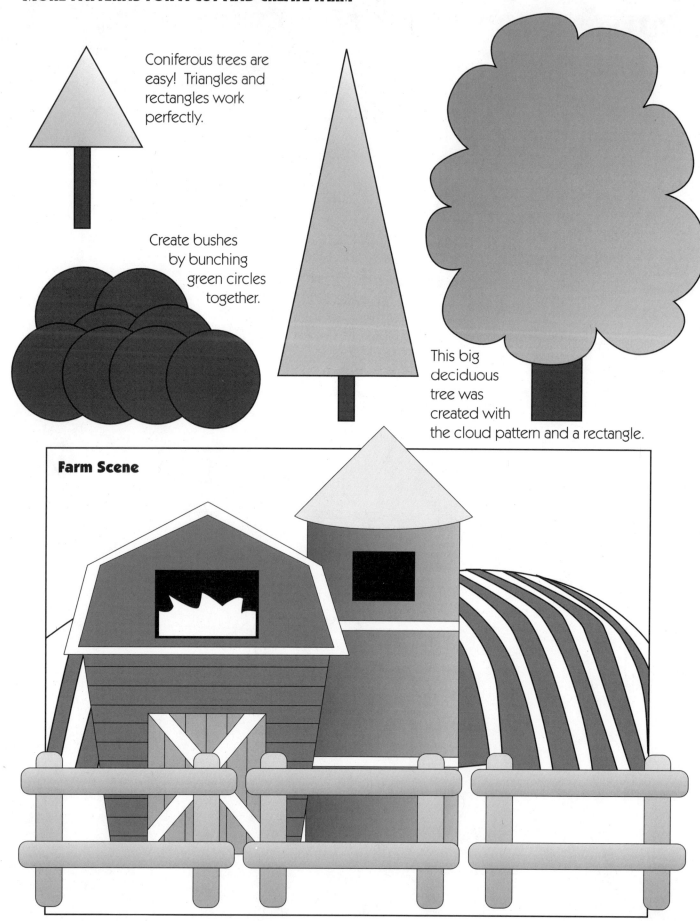

Coniferous trees are easy! Triangles and rectangles work perfectly.

Create bushes by bunching green circles together.

This big deciduous tree was created with the cloud pattern and a rectangle.

Farm Scene